BETH MOORE

ALL MY KNOTTED-UP LIFE

A MEMOIR

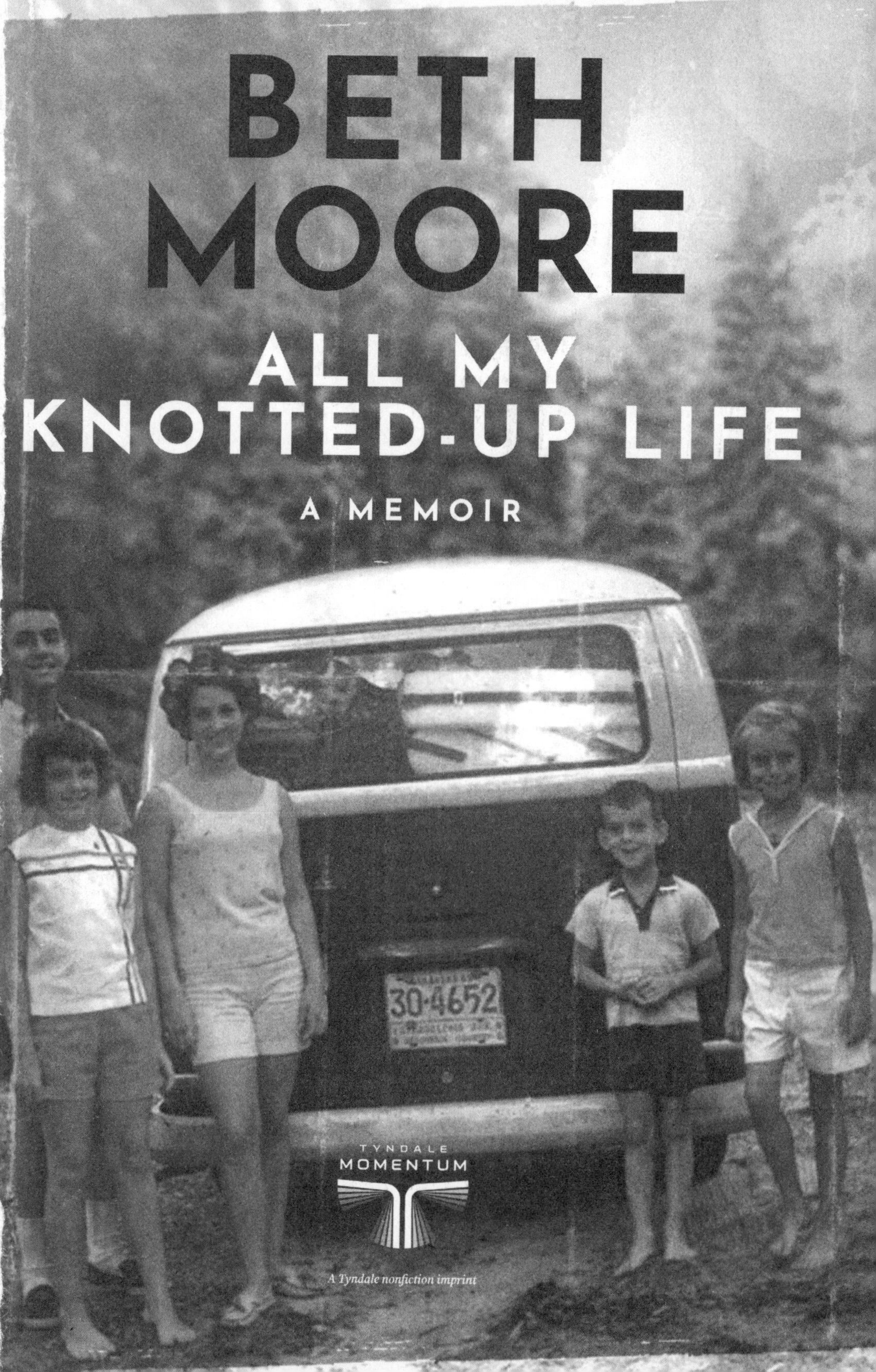

TYNDALE
MOMENTUM

A Tyndale nonfiction imprint

Visit Tyndale online at tyndale.com.

Visit Tyndale Momentum online at tyndalemomentum.com.

Visit Beth Moore online at lproof.org.

Tyndale, Tyndale's quill logo, *Tyndale Momentum*, and the Tyndale Momentum logo are registered trademarks of Tyndale House Ministries. Tyndale Momentum is a nonfiction imprint of Tyndale House Publishers, Carol Stream, Illinois.

All My Knotted-Up Life: A Memoir

Designed by Jacqueline L. Nuñez

Edited by Kathryn S. Olson

Unless otherwise indicated, all Scripture quotations are taken from the Christian Standard Bible,® copyright © 2017 by Holman Bible Publishers. Used by permission. Christian Standard Bible® and CSB® are federally registered trademarks of Holman Bible Publishers.

Scripture quotations marked KJV are taken from the *Holy Bible*, King James Version.

Scripture quotations marked NIV are taken from the Holy Bible, *New International Version,*® *NIV.*® Copyright © 1973, 1978, 1984, 2011 by Biblica, Inc.® Used by permission. All rights reserved worldwide.

For information about special discounts for bulk purchases, please contact Tyndale House Publishers at csresponse@tyndale.com, or call 1-855-277-9400.

Library of Congress Cataloging-in-Publication Data

A catalog record for this book is available from the Library of Congress.

ISBN 978-1-4964-7267-0

Printed in the United States of America

29	28	27	26	25	24	23
7	6	5	4	3	2	1

To Keith:
Through the fire,
through the flood,
God has been faithful to us.
I love you.

With deep gratitude to my siblings,
in the order of appearance on the cover,
Wayne, Gay, Sandra, and Tony.
I do not take lightly your willingness
to allow me to invite a public view
into my corner of our private lives.
I love you all.

A NOTE FROM THE AUTHOR

THE BURDEN IN TELLING OUR INDIVIDUAL STORY is ironically the same thing that made it bearable: we were not alone in it. Perhaps we felt we were, but the truth is, the threads of other people's lives are inevitably knotted into ours even if only by their conspicuous absence. Who, after all, plays a bigger part in our story than one who—whether by sickness, injury, dozing, distraction, occupation, brokenness, divorce, or death—didn't show up? Every life story entails a community of individuals who share one precarious common denominator in the narrative: *you*. Good or bad, *you*. Right or wrong, *you*. The responsibility is immense and, to anyone with a whit of sense, terribly intimidating.

I love a story told, and I love the actual storytelling, but I have not been in a hurry to write a memoir. I think I've been waiting for everything to work out neatly and cleanly. Sensibly. Politely. You hold this book in your hands in large part because I gave up on that. But in a way, the giving up feels more like relief than resignation. I suppose I've also been scared to see the pieces of my story tied together. Scared to discover that what made the whole of it hardest of all was me.

I've waited to write a memoir until my reasons to do so finally exceeded my reasons to refrain. Time had to pass. People had to pass. Others had to age enough to no longer care much what people think. I've worried about hurting people. I've wondered if the kinder thing to do for those who have known my family might be to leave them with better impressions. I lament that telling my story might imply more about the experiences of my family members than either they or I would wish. I've asked their permission and received their blessing and tried my best to leave the most vulnerable parts of their stories to them, but I'm not blind to the cost of showing up in someone else's book. I wince knowing that a story, once told, cannot be untold.

I've attempted, by the grace of God, to untie some knots in these pages. Several of these knots I've kept clenched in a sweaty fist all my life. They needed air and light perhaps even more than understanding. The same distance that can clarify a story can also cloud it. The trick in writing a memoir is knowing which is which. Am I ready to tell it because it is clearer now or because it is less clear? My deep hope, my determined intention, is the former, but the lens of human perception is inevitably impaired.

Few things are more unnerving than writing a memoir of your life with an unknown measure of it yet unlived. For instance, what if the good parts go belly-up before the book even hits a shelf? Publishing a book is always an act of faith. It's a way of saying, "Dear Reader, here is what I'm thinking right now—what I believe to be true and long to be of value to you—but would you forgive me and not hold it against the God of whom I speak if time or divine Providence proves me wrong or woefully deficient?"

And now, if you'll entrust to me a bit of your time, I'll entrust to you a bit of my story.

PROLOGUE

DON'T LET GO. Whatever you do, don't let go. I crumpled my eyelids in two tight knots then cracked them open enough to get my bearings. The current was milky with sand like someone had topped off a big glass of water with a splash of buttermilk. A clod of seaweed grazed my forehead then tumbled off my nose, and water shot through my head, foamy and thick with brine, meeting no apparent barrier and whirlpooling between my ringing ears.

Forcing an eyeshot behind me, I caught sight of my dad's foot. His skin appeared translucent beneath the water, the noon sun turning his purple veins an anemic lilac. We'd been standing beside one another in the surf seconds earlier. We'd inched further out without even moving somehow. The watermark reached the waist of my red one-piece, but he was little more than knee deep. And he was my dad. He'd know where to stop. I dangled my hands just below the surface, palms forward and fingers outstretched, making rivulets in the curl of the calm waves, dazzled by their constancy. This was my maiden voyage to the sea, the first I'd felt the curious tickle of a shifting floor of sand between my toes.

Then, out of nowhere, I was underwater. My arms were instantly taut, elbowless, jerking my shoulders until they swore they'd snap. *Grab me, Dad, before I let go.* My fingers were laced around his right ankle, knuckles locked. My spine stretched into a thin strip of taffy. At the pull of an unheard trigger, I was a bullet of skin clinging to the end of a barrel, begging not to be shot out to sea.

As swiftly as the undertow had sucked my feet out from under me, the current shifted and I swung around, unbending, like the second hand of a clock dropping from 12 to 6, face planted in the sand. My father's sudden yank on my arms snapped my hand-lock from his ankle and I swung like a rag doll to my feet, coughing up a salt mine, a mud-pie patch over one eye. I bit my lip to keep from crying.

I don't remember what Dad said. Perhaps something like, "You're okay. You're okay." It would have been true enough. My arms were limp, but they weren't torn away from my shoulders the way I'd pictured. No sea monsters had managed to drive me out to the open sea and into the gullets of great fish with ten-inch teeth. But *something* had happened, and I wanted to know what. I wanted to know what took him so long. I wanted to know if it scared him that the water tried to swallow me. And I wanted him to say he was sorry, even if he couldn't have helped it. He never knew I had any such questions. I couldn't form a word.

I was turned over to my mother, who was perched on a rusty blue and green web-strap chair under a beach umbrella to shield her fair skin and her seventy-seven-year-old mother from the unfiltered rays of the Florida sun. She gently faced me forward and held me securely between her knees, still chatting with Nanny. Something about my cousin Steedy Boy. He sure was going to be tall, they agreed. The frazzled edge of a strap on the folding chair scratched and bit at the back of my leg.

"Reckon does he have a girlfriend?" My grandmother loved knowing that kind of thing. I liked that about her. I wouldn't have minded knowing the answer myself, just not that very minute.

"Well, I don't know," Mom replied to Nanny. "You'll have to ask him."

"Well, I'm asking you."

"Well, Mother, I don't know."

"Well, *why* don't you know?"

My teeth chattered so hard I thought they'd crack, and my throat stung from the saltwater rush like a potato peeler had been taken to it. As Mom toweled off my shivering six-year-old frame, she asked quizzically, "You cold, honey?" I paused a moment trying to figure out if, somewhere beneath the scared, I was just plain-old ordinary cold. Maybe so. I nodded. She rubbed my arms briskly with a turquoise towel that had a blue and yellow turtle on it. "Let me warm you up!" I still couldn't get a word out. I don't know why, exactly. She would have let me tell her that I thought I was drowning. She wouldn't have made me feel silly. She would have pulled me into her lap and let me cry, and I just know she'd have been hopping mad at my dad. But I couldn't tell her any of it. Never did. My grandmother's question just hung in the air. "Well, why don't you know?"

CHAPTER ONE

WE WERE RIVER PEOPLE. River people don't have any business going to the sea. The state of Arkansas is an innard in the abdomen of North America, a gallbladder maybe or a spleen. Our arteries pool with visible edges. Arkansas waters are crossable, bridgeable, cushioned on every bank. My hometown of Arkadelphia rests at the bumpy toes of the Ouachita Mountains where two rivers converge. The Ouachita, some six hundred miles total, gathers up the shorter Caddo just north of town, and together they run green and curvy down the city's east side on their lazy way to Louisiana.

With my dad's recent purchase of a blue and white Volkswagen bus, we Greens finally had a vehicle with a wide enough mouth for all eight of us. Since we all fit, why not drive for days on end, packed tighter than my great-grandmother Miss Ruthie's chewing tobacco, from our small college town all the way to our cousins in north Florida?

"What's a few more miles?" Dad said, taking a red felt-tip to the map and tracing an additional eight-hour jaunt due south to Miami Beach. He, Major Albert B. Green, took charge of the wheel. My mother, Esther Aletha Rountree Green, rode shotgun, with my four-year-old brother, Tony, wiggling like a caged spider monkey between them.

My maternal grandmother, Minnie Ola Rountree, whom we called Nanny, took a lion's share of the middle seat. She was not a small woman, swore she never had been nor did I ever want her to be. Nanny was squooshy, ample-bosomed, pillowy for napping against. The middle seat was a slightly abbreviated version of the back bench seat, and Nanny bounced on its wealth of springs between my nine-year-old sister, Gay, and me. Born three years apart, we two Green girls were thick as thieves and would prove to be precisely as trustworthy.

Named Aletha Gay after our mom, she favored her in appearance, sharing her pecan-brown hair, fair skin, and fetching swathe of freckles across her cheeks. I, the lone blonde in the family, was told from the time I could walk that I favored a different wing of the family. In an era when laboring moms were knocked out for delivery, I came with a bit of a rush, causing my mom to forego the usual protocol and keeping her wide awake for every contraction. Still woozy-headed from the furious ordeal, she took one look at me and bellowed with clear astonishment, "She looks just like my brother-in-law!" This declaration invited all manner of mischief from the nursing staff, who made eyes at her when my dad visited the hospital then winked at her when he came to drive us home.

Two years later, Tony came along looking a good bit more like

Dad and the singular one of us born in our hometown. Gay and I were the only built-in playmates the poor little guy had. He could, therefore, either play what we were playing or play alone. Since we mostly played dolls and he refused to be shut out, he had no recourse but to join us. Tony possessed the maternal touch of a Mack truck, so we assigned him a lesser-cherished baby doll and one durable enough to withstand him. He promptly stuck it all the way to the toe of a long white sock of Dad's and carried it around by the ribbed cuff each time we played. Watching him knock it clumsily against table legs, doorframes, and tree trunks day in and day out caused Gay and me considerable consternation.

Tony was the baby of a three-generation family well-versed in children, so he was warmly humored. "Whatcha got there, Tony?" the adults and big kids would ask. "Oh, this old thing?" he'd say, shrugging his bony little shoulders. "Just a plain ole doll." This was, henceforth, the name it bore. We were forbidden to take any toys bigger than our palms on our summer vacation in the VW bus. One can't be entirely certain that Dad hadn't contrived such a rule in hopes of leaving Plain Ole Doll home in a sock where he believed it belonged. Luckily, two Matchbox cars fit perfectly in Tony's palms, so he made motor sounds and crash noises every waking moment of the trip.

Since Tony's head only popped into view when we hit a pot-hole, Nanny, who'd never procured a license nor once been behind a wheel, had a clear view to aid my father vociferously in his driving from her perch in the middle seat. Her second advantage was full range of motion to swat anyone who proved worthy of it. Old as she was, she aimed more than struck, so the sibling next to the offender may as well have been complicit. Whoever coined the idiom *hitting two birds with one stone* was looking square at the arm of my nanny. The generous amount of flesh that hung from her upper arm flapped winglike when she swung. I figure this was the secret to her momentum.

Riding caboose in the VW bus were the oldest two of us five Green kids. My sister, Sandra, was an exotic eighteen. She knew how to do good hair and makeup, and she had a college-aged boyfriend. Gay and I were in awe of her and had high hopes of her turning out to be deliciously scandalous. She never delivered, but we set the bar low enough for scandal that any drama at all satisfied, and if the Greens were good at anything, it was drama. Next to her in the back seat was my dreamy big brother, Wayne. He was fourteen, the uncontested crush of my entire young life, and through my hazel eyes, Paul McCartney's identical twin. And he was musical. Who on earth would think this a coincidence? Sandra and Wayne were inarguably in their prime because they knew how to dance. They could put a stack of 45s on the record player at home, shake and swing like they were on Dick Clark, then flip those records over and do it all again to another set of songs. They may as well have been hippies.

We were told to pack light, so a mishmash of no less than ten pieces of luggage was strapped hillbilly-like to the top of the van alongside our brand-new tent from the Sears and Roebuck, still in its packaging. None of us had ever camped before except the major, of course, on battlefields in World War II and Korea, though we hoped for a different ambience. Motel expenses for a voluminous family on summer vacation were out of the question on an Army budget. Our kind of people didn't take destination vacations anyhow. We only went to see relatives on account of cheaper food and lodging. It wasn't until much later, after we moved to Houston, that I'd ever hear anyone say, "We're going snow skiing for spring break." *What kin live there?* "Who's Ken?" they'd say. *I didn't say Ken. I said kin. Your relatives.* Texans didn't have the vocabulary God gave a groundhog. "Well, none," they'd say. *Well, why are you going?* "To ski," they'd say.

Since I have no vivid memory when this wasn't so, I don't think it's too soon to say that Albert and Aletha were not as fond of one another as one might hope on a two-week vacation or, for that matter, what would turn out to be a fifty-something-year-long marriage. I could offer a good many reasons why this was true, but for now, only one is needful: my father drove with both feet, his right sole on the accelerator and his left on the brake, even when he was privileged to be at the wheel of an automatic.

The erratic spasms of Dad's two-foot driving made a catnap particularly challenging for passengers on a protracted trip. My mother was the anxious type, at which I, a woman of like ilk, choose to cast no stone. I mean only to paint the picture of my parents, Albert and Aletha, in the front seat of a VW bus for hours. She kept her left arm stretched over my little brother at all times and her right hand braced on the dashboard with a lit cigarette between her index and middle fingers, catching a drag when catch could. And catch always could.

I was raised in a cloudy pillar by day and a lighter by night. To this day, I nurse a fondness for the sound of a match head combusting against the striking strip of a small rectangular box— *tet-szzzzoooo* like a petite bottle rocket on the Fourth of July—and for the pitchy quick-fading scent of sulfur dioxide.

The real work on that summer vacation began when we stopped for the night at the Fort Walton Beach campsite. I suspect saving the expense of motel stays might not have been the solitary reason for the tent purchase. My cousins were campers in the same way ants are insects. They were the sort that could have started a fire rubbing dandelions together, and lost in a forest, weeks of wild berries, grasshoppers, and deer milk would have left them no less robust.

We were more the Piggly Wiggly type. It was never said, "How hard could putting up a tent be?" But what did go without saying was that my father never missed a chance to compete, and my uncle, whom we'd see shortly, was a formidable foe. He was the only one in the entire extended family whose record in the armed services came close to Dad's, and let no one suppose that a competition's being "friendly" makes it a whit less serious. Dad didn't use a lot of profanity, but he had a way of making perfectly respectable slang words sound brazen. He found little aid from the written instructions that came with the tent packaging and what appeared to be no aid at all from the audible instructions that came with Nanny. On the average day, an impressive number of Nanny's sentences began with the words *Well, why don't you . . . ?* On this trip, as far as I could tell, she was clocking at a record 98 percent.

Dad was tricolored by now, his face deep red against that one narrow strip of white in a head full of hair that was otherwise the color of cocoa. I'd always thought that one shock of white looked like someone dribbled a tablespoon of trimming paint on his head and, feeling something wet, he'd run his little finger from forehead to crown to wipe it off. I'd been wrong all along. It was as clear as a bell now exactly what it looked like: a single strike of lightning. This was not so much frightening as it was factual.

While Dad tried to figure out which side of the tent was the top, Mom emptied half a carton of Pall Malls. The more he huffed, the more she puffed. The rest of us coped with the taxing assemblage in our own ways. Wayne stood by wide-eyed, fidgeting with an edge of the canvas, scared to help and scared not to. Any second, Dad was going to say, "Are you just going to stand there?" I suspect this quickly approaching inevitability is why Sandra suddenly volunteered to walk Gay to the campground restrooms. Tony threw rocks, which lessened neither the huffing nor the puffing, and I sucked my usual two fingers and stared at the night sky, wondering why Florida had no stars. We had stars in Arkansas.

Having finally triumphed over the tent pegs, Dad entered through the zippered door and was swallowed whole by nylon. A great flailing commenced, a ghost thrashing. Somewhere near the apparition's rotating head, the top end of a tent pole searched wretchedly for a point until it was found and affixed. Dad emerged like a slathered newborn from a heavy-labored nylon womb.

Each of us was handed an olive-green air mattress to blow up for our beds. Nanny, being elderly and all, got both an air mattress and a cot to set it on. There is an art to squeezing the mattress valve open while you blow through it that exceeds the mastery of small children. Despite the loudest of efforts, Tony's lips never did seal around the valve, meaning he primarily spit on his mattress. What was left dry, he likely wet during the night. I puffed a few thimblefuls of air into the pillow compartment of mine and grew dramatically faint. By the time we'd wrangled eight mattresses and a cot inside the tent and crawled in for the night, the choppy asthmatic breaths of oxygen-deprived blowers punctured the thick, steamy air.

● ● ●

Family is a heck of a thing, fierce and frightful. There we are, all zipped up inside the unknown together and not always voluntarily. It can be dark in there, trying to get through the night. We can feel utterly alone, singular and isolated, while crushed and crowded and so close in body that our sweat mingles and we inhale what they exhale, unfiltered. We want to touch, to hold hands, on our own terms, which is our right and ought to be our right, but most times we don't. We go from knowing each other better than we know ourselves, to barely sure if we know each other at all, to precisely sure that we don't. And truth be told, we don't know one another in the same way outsiders might. We know too much to know each other.

Reasonable allowances have to be made amid such nearness. We want to be known but not memorized as if we cannot change. Family has a way of freezing its constituents in time, for better or for worse, confident that what was true twenty years ago is true now and will be true in twenty more. Unchecked, we lose sight of one another's otherness. We're amoebas, constantly swallowing one another or splitting off, simultaneously demanding singularity and intimacy.

These are my people. My original loves, my flesh and my bones. I know their jokes. I know their quirks. We have the same noses. Different slices of the same secrets are on our plates. We've survived the same blows. We speak in strange tongues, syllables of a run-on sentence that began in our infancies, untranslatable to casual visitors.

All my knotted-up life I've longed for the sanity and simplicity of knowing who's good and who's bad. I've wanted to know this about myself as much as anyone. I needed God to clean up the mess, divide the room, sort the mail so all of us can just get on with it and be who we are. Go where we're bent. This was not theological. It was strictly relational. God could do what he wanted with eternity. I was just trying to make it here in the meantime, and what I thought would help me make it was for people to be one thing or the other, good or bad. Keep it simple. As benevolent as he has been in a myriad of ways, God has remained aloof on this uncomplicated request.

Take my dad's grandmother, Miss Ruthie, for example. She was a hard woman to watch, chewing all that tobacco. At times the foaming saliva was as thick and brown as molasses and, instead of committing to the task with a resolute and plosive *puh*, she seemed perfectly happy to let it hang. A quarter teaspoon would suspend from her lower lip like it had no place to go. She held onto her spit can like an old country preacher hanging on to his King James. If she got up, she carried it around with her, sloshing. By *it*, I mean the spit can, not that a Bible can't slosh on occasion. She stuck the whole thing in a brown paper bag with the edges rolled down like nobody would know what was in it. I never once saw her without her hair in a tight knot right on top of her head like a large white spool. I cannot think the topknot was unrelated to the spit can. No woman wants her hair dangling in her chaw.

This was Miss Ruthie, plain as day. We knew all we needed to know about her. She was one thing, not two. Then my brother Wayne told me, "I spent the night with Miss Ruthie one time, and when she took all those pins out of her hair and leaned forward in her chair to brush it, her hair fell all the way to the floor, silky and beautiful. I was fascinated." My whole family—well, for the most part—is like this. Spitting in a can, all spool-headed, one minute. Sleek and lovely and mesmerizing the next.

That I find measurable security in clean-cut categories, in jet black and blood red and bleached white, explains why most of my life has been a slow baptism in the lukewarm waters of a silty gray Jordan.

● ● ●

I'm not sure how many of us had fallen asleep when the first clap of thunder came, but my mother shot up from her air mattress like she'd been electrified. The next strip of lightning was a white-hot fillet knife, severing the starless tarp over Fort Walton Beach, dumping a pent-up lake right on top of us.

In our family, fear was a core value. We were tutored and tested on it, unapologetically indoctrinated on how to live life terrified out of our minds, hypervigilant against every threat because one truth was truer than all other truths: life would kill you. No matter what we were in the middle of doing, be it showering or making cinnamon toast, when a thunderstorm hit, everybody in the house had to scurry to the nearest spot to sit and prop our feet up, and God help you if your nearest place was next to a window. You'd be dead, seared to charcoal, in seconds, and the sight of you would scar the rest of us for life. The propping of the feet was an utmost priority because when—not if—lightning struck the house, anyone with sole of feet on wood of floor would perish. This fact was also somehow connected to why we couldn't turn a light switch on and off with one hand while holding a glass of water in the other.

The marvel of our Sears and Roebuck tent was that, in the brief wake of a long, laborious assembly, it disassembled with remarkable ease. There was no waiting around to watch the full collapse, however. Not with Mom yelling the way she was. She bellowed with such volume for us to *run!* to the VW that it's a wonder every camper within a thousand square feet didn't beat us to it. Nanny's mouth ran much faster than her legs, so she put it to use advancing our gait from behind. "Git! Didn't I say git? I did! I said git!" And we did.

To spare her dignity, I tried not to stare at Nanny once she made it into the van. She couldn't help that her hair was feathery to start with and, now that it was wet, she appeared not to have hair one. The way I knew her hair was feathery is because, every time Mom teased Nanny's hair to give it a little height, she'd say, "If your hair wasn't suh feathery . . ."

I tried to look straight ahead and mind my own affairs, only to catch a glimpse of Dad's hair in the rearview mirror. The downpour had caused his streak of lightning to slide from the top of his forehead to his eyebrow in a near perfect diagonal, dripping curiously at the tip end. He'd soon pull out his small plastic comb and correct it, but I resolved to ponder the sight for some time.

He slipped the bus into reverse and we sped away from a family-size tent, eight air mattresses, and one cot like we'd never known them. By sheer divine mercy, we happened on an open-all-night diner near Fort Walton Beach and took refuge there until the storm passed and the sun winked sleepily from the east. The diner could've used a good sweeping, but years of well-peppered hamburger meat and salty eggs and bacon sizzling on the stainless-steel grill had glazed the walls, tables, and chairs with such a layer of grease that the whole place smelled like we'd died and gone to heaven. Half a dozen crinkle-cut fries were scattered on the floor, but they looked like they'd been pretty good at some point.

Dad's mood had not improved, but the handwriting was on the wall by way of a thumbtacked menu. No way was this tent-worn family not going to eat. He pulled out his wallet and thumbed through a modest vacation's worth of dollar bills, and we kids glanced at one another with glee. He didn't say yes, but Dad's yes was when he didn't say no. We ordered the bare minimum straight from the cook. No one dared say the word *Coca-Cola*, let alone *chocolate shake*. We knew we were on our benefactor's last nerve. By the time our stomachs were full, we were sleepy and grouchy and bored, so Tony, Gay, and I had little choice but to amuse ourselves by licking the grape and strawberry jelly out of the little packets on the tables. Those were free.

The subject was bound to come up at some point and this was as good a time as any.

"I shoulda flown," Nanny said, perturbed, scooting the metal chair back from the Formica table and folding her arms across her chest. When Nanny made a definitive statement, she ended it by jutting out her jaw and swallowing her upper lip with her lower lip. This was sign language for *That's all there is to it.*

Mom jumped right in like she'd been waiting for it all day. "Flown? Momma, have you forgotten what a lather you got yourself into the last time you flew?"

"When?"

"Two years ago when you flew to Florida!"

"I don't 'member no lather."

"What do you mean, you don't remember? You don't remember packing your burial dress in your suitcase?"

"Wadn't no lather to it. Puredee common sense. I see it ain't as common as it orta be."

Mom rubbed her head.

Dad had all but turned his back to his kin by then, like we hadn't all come in together. When my father's face was only a little flushed, you could see—that is, if you knew what you were looking for—that place where they patched the left side of his face, right there between his cheekbone and his nose, after he took a bullet early in World War II. If it didn't get a good gush of blood supply, it stayed gray, looking just like Silly Putty, like it knew it belonged on a different cheek.

In my family we rightly called any private part of the body *the bunny.* We did not say *bottom,* and we certainly did not say *butt.* Well, all but Tony, who continually spelled it out loud just because he was naughty, but since he spelled it "b-o-t-t," he didn't get fussed at. Me and Gay loved snickering about how Dad's bunny was on his face, especially when we were in trouble. Mind you, I didn't get in much trouble because I was "overly sensitive" and scared of him, but Gay wasn't scared of the devil. She stayed in a fair amount of trouble on account of her mouth, but whispering "Bunny Face" behind his back was no small consolation.

Mom and Nanny were still going at it in the all-night diner. Now, there was no one on earth my momma loved more than my nanny, but she likely knew that, if she didn't react to Nanny smarting off that she should've flown to Florida, Dad would, and then it would go from a harmless argument to something that wasn't. Everybody knows in-laws can't get away with saying what blood can.

"Who would think an old woman ort not to take a buryin' dress?" Nanny let her voice tremble a bit and feigned a most stricken look, like her feet were already resting lifeless in a casket. "My heart could give out at any time."

"Minnie Rountree," my mother said, "you know good and well taking that burial dress had nothing to do with you being an old woman. Had nothing to do with your heart, either. You said it yourself. You packed your burial dress in the likely case the Cubans planned to hijack the plane."

Things like this had to play out in my mind so I could make sense of them. I guessed the hijackers would bury Nanny in Cuba, and I wasn't sure where that was, but I knew it was a long way from Arkadelphia. I further guessed they'd fetch her burial dress out of her suitcase and put it on her before they put her in the ground in a Cuban casket.

"Load up!" Dad had gone outside and taken a good look at the sky and stuck his head back through the doorway, motioning for us. We were a disheveled bunch and red-eyed, climbing back into the VW bus. Our tires bumped and splashed through wide puddles left by the night storm as we made our way back to the campsite. There was no rescuing the tent. This was strictly a recovery mission. Dad pulled out the cot first, then all eight air mattresses, and that's when we little kids saved the day. We hopped from one mattress to the next, marching on them, stomping on them, and turning somersaults on them with great enthusiasm while those over five feet tall held the nozzles open so they'd deflate. According to my oldest sister, Dad didn't bother with the formality of folding the tent. He wadded it up in a big hunk, then roped it to the back with a bungee cord. Sandra declared it was so heavy that every time we hit a bump, the back fender dragged on the pavement.

We drove just like that all the way into the open arms of our cousins, who had a small and spectacularly wonderful little place by the lake. We were Arkansans. We understood lakes. We had a blissful three days with our Rountree cousins whether Aunt Jewel could cook a decent pancake or not. We also managed to make it to Miami, that fast and furious town of renown, though by this time, all hopes of cruising proudly down its palm-lined boulevards proved mockingly vain. The alternator went out on our brand-new blue and white Volkswagen bus, and until we could get to a mechanic who'd extend credit, Sandra and Wayne were enlisted to push it while Dad started it. This was understandably humiliating to them both and untoward for exotics. From the middle seat directly behind Dad, I intuited, young though I was, his pinch-lipped disappointment in their lack of zeal. I tried to sit light on the seat in case it helped. Sandra's detailed memory of the way the tent was bunched up on the back came on account of it not being all that easy to find a good place to push.

The last stop on our summer vacation was the parking lot of the Sears and Roebuck. Dad, having retrieved his purchase from the bumper of the bus, was seen marching as to war through the thick glass doors with a vinyl tent big enough for eight wadded up in his arms, window flaps dangling at his knees. Our home away from home was returned replete with leaves, sand, and a brisk request for a refund. With one last push, we made it up the hill to a modest red-brick dwelling on the outskirts of our small, familiar town.

Before Nanny could plant her foot steady on the concrete beneath the carport, Mom was turning on the water kettle, Dad was in the bathroom with a newspaper, Sandra was calling her boyfriend, Wayne was playing the piano, Gay was riding her bike, and Tony had a dog by the tail. And I? Well, I was twirling around on the burlap-bag swing hanging from the strong arm of an Arkansas pine, its golden-brown needles between my toes.

CHAPTER TWO

MOM SAID THE REASON WE WERE MOVING from the hill to the Ligon house on Twelfth Street was that driving us kids back and forth to town all day long to school and every other activity known to man was driving her batty. All the back and forth, what Mom called *taxi driving* to us kids who'd never seen a taxi, might not have been as bad if Mom bought more than fifty cents' worth of gas at a time. I cast no blame for this because I figure she only had fifty cents, the way she was always digging in her pocketbook for change, which struck me as strange, because why else would anyone leave the hill except to move into a mansion?

To Gay, Tony, and me, this appeared to be exactly what we were doing since it was three whole rooms bigger. We'd also never heard a house called by a name before, so that had to mean it was fancy. "We're moving to the Ligon house," my parents would say. "The Greens have bought the Ligon house," the neighbors would say. It was Tudor style with a wealth of windows and with white trim accenting two front-facing gables, one a smaller version of the other, beneath a steeply pitched green roof. Wrapped around it were red bricks that looked like they'd been left in the toaster on purpose till they were nearly brown. We were told the place was called the Ligon house because Mrs. Ligon had lived there. This explanation was never satisfactory for the most obvious of reasons. Why weren't the people buying our house on the hill moving into *the Green house*? And why hadn't we ever called the dilapidated place next to us on the hill *the Rountree house* instead of *the old house*? Folks didn't treat houses the same.

I guessed we were rich now since Sandra, going on twenty, had gotten married, and Dad had retired from the Army and been hired as the manager of the Royal Theater on Main Street and the SkyVue Drive-In out on Highway 67. The whole town knew because he'd made the *Siftings Herald*. Still, the move was no improvement the way I saw it. We were leaving all that breathing space—and walking distance to the Caddo River, where we could dig crawdads out of the mud—in order to live on a city block where Wayne could walk straight across the street to the high school.

"That's not all. The primary school and elementary are right around the corner, too." Mom laid it on thick as molasses there in the kitchen, Nanny looking dubious with her hands in oven mitts waiting for a casserole to bubble. A keen observer could regularly tell what Nanny thought about something by the position of her elbows when her hands were on her hips. If they were pointed behind her, she was fine enough with it, but if they were straight out to the sides like bat wings, she was smelling a rat.

"And Tony's about to go to primary and Beth, elementary, and the junior high where Gay'll go next year is only a block or two further."

If I hadn't known better, I'd have sworn she looked glad we'd soon all be in school.

"Think how we'll be able to play indoors," Gay commented, looking on the bright side.

Who wanted to? Out on the hill, we shot outside the minute we gulped down the sweet milk from our cereal bowls, and if we didn't have school, we played all over that hill for hours on end with unbrushed teeth and crusty milk mustaches, skittering over spiny green balls of sweet gums and the pointy brown cones of pines until the soles of our feet were as tough as whitleather, only darkening the door for snacks. This we did out of preference and also because Nanny would poke us with the needly end of the broom the second we set down our bowls and say, "Scat on outta here or I'll give you something to do." Nanny never wanted a person to do something fun, not even Pappaw, my dad's dad.

Mammaw was long dead and, to hear it told, nobody blamed her. She'd run Green's Café for years by herself. "Yep, worked herself into a nub until she give up and died quick as Christmas of the cancers," people would say. And whoever else was listening would nod and say, "Uh-huh."

Even though Pappaw was at least a decade Nanny's junior, he was always poorly. She'd hear his old pickup clanging up the hill, gears screeching, and she'd say, "Well, here's company, and I reckon that old man'll sit here like a knot on a log and expect me to wait on him all day like I don't have a form thing to do, and right in time for my stories." Nobody with any sense got between Nanny and *Guiding Light* and *The Edge of Night*. If we peeked our heads through the door while she and Mom were in front of the

TV with their bread-and-butter fold-overs, they'd shout the word *out!* in one voice.

Pappaw might show up anytime of the week, but he showed up like clockwork on Fridays if Ouachita Baptist University right below us was having a home football game. Small-town football got everybody's blood flowing. Dad and Pappaw would carry lawn chairs from the carport over to the edge of the hill, set them up amid the trees, and watch the football game plain as day for free like they were kings in a skybox. We kids would run circles around them, stealing unshelled peanuts by the handfuls from their brown paper sacks, energized into frenzies by the blaring sounds of announcers calling plays, refs whistling, and bands playing.

Now, Pappaw watched the game with only one eye—not because he wanted to, but because he'd lost the other one to lye soap. He always wore a pair of glasses that had a clear lens on one side and a cloudy lens on the other so you couldn't see what was missing, but I saw it anyway. I would testify to anyone who'd listen that I'd beheld it and it wasn't that bad.

"The eye isn't there, is all." I'd pause and let the thought settle on them, then say, "Everything else is."

His skin was sunk in and hollowed out like someone had taken an ice cream scoop to it but the place where there should've been an eye was just a straight half-inch strip of pink, long ago sewn together. No eyelashes, but I hadn't been expecting any. They were sparse on his good eye.

Gay and I reasoned it like a riddle. "What would you have if you took Popeye from the television set, growed him old, and stoled his spinach?"

"Well," we said, "you'd have Pappaw."

We refused to be sad about it because we'd never gotten to know his bad eye anyway, and he could still watch the Ouachita

Tigers play and throw peanut shells at us kids with his good eye. But Nanny said, "It ain't helped his drivin' none."

The important thing was that being one-eyed hadn't hurt Pappaw's treehouse-building. I don't care who had a finer house or a finer car with a fuller tank of gas, no one could boast a better treehouse than the one Dad and Pappaw had built out back for us kids. They'd wedged it between a couple of thick oaks, resting its considerable weight on muscular branches. They'd cut squares out of the side boards for windows and built a hatch door into the floor, the latter of which was met by a fair measure of disapproval from Nanny.

"Hope them old pair a fools'll be happy when these young'uns break their necks."

We three climbed in and out of that treehouse ten times a day. Gay played with me happy as could be, acting like I was fun and not a bit a bother. She was only mean when Megen Riley, who lived right down the hill behind us, came up acting starry-eyed about her. Megen was Tony's age and his best playmate, but her mother didn't make her take a nap like our mother made Tony, so if Tony was unavailable, she was left with us. I wouldn't have minded this mix except that two's company and three's a crowd, causing them, on occasion, to hole up in the treehouse, latch the trapdoor, and refuse to let me in. The worst part was how they'd play Beatles' wives just like Gay and I always played, and they'd claim the two best ones.

"What about me?" I'd plead from down below.

"You can be Ringo's wife," they'd shout from above. I didn't want to be Ringo's wife. I never had to be Ringo's wife except when Megen Riley was over.

"George's then!"

I didn't want to be George's wife either.

"Well, be the maid then."

Meaner than snakes is what they were. I would sit cross-legged below in a pout, mildly comforted that Megen, young as she was, didn't get half the words to the songs right.

I suspected Gay's galling partiality had something to do with Megen getting to have a real pool in her backyard on account of being an only child. This seemed an unnecessary gesture since we got to swim over there often anyway because Mrs. Riley was so nice. After all, she saved my life.

In my family, you didn't get to do a whole lot of tattling. The tattletale was worse than the tattled-on any day, which seemed a shame to me. Simply put, Nanny didn't want to hear it and Mom was taking a five-minute nap, so they were no help at all. Dad was hardly ever home in the daylight, but we wouldn't have tattled to him anyway or he'd wag the slack end of the belt he was wearing as his way of signaling, "Do you want a whuppin'?"

"Why would *anybody* want a whuppin'?" was what I always wanted to ask.

So here's how Mrs. Riley happened to save my life. When Gay and Megen were in the treehouse again and wouldn't let me in, I was left with no choice but to take the matter into my own hands. My arms and legs were as spindly as a chimp's, Nanny said, and I could climb like one. I grabbed a low branch on an adjacent tree with both hands and cupped my feet on the trunk, curling my toes into the bark and inching my way up, quiet and stealth-like, until I was level with the treehouse. It was a superb spot for eavesdropping, and I don't mind saying, I heard an earful. All of a sudden, so did Mrs. Riley. The branch I was perched on snapped so loud, someone may as well have lit a firecracker. The limb hit the ground first and I followed it posthaste, sprawling flat on my back, my lungs expelling air like a popped balloon.

Before I could gather enough oxygen to emit the first wail, Mrs. Riley already had me in her tanned arms, hollering, "Letha!" and running toward the house with my feet dangling at her shins and my chin curved over her shoulder. By this time, my chest was lurching, and according to Nanny, I was "crying loud like she was near kilt," and Mom was swinging the door wide open and motioning toward the couch. Soon Gay and Megen showed up, looking small and stricken and terribly sorry, staring at me "near kilt" on the couch. I fluttered my eyes and tried to roll them back in my head. Nanny, Mrs. Riley, and Mom were fussing over me, checking my arms and legs.

"Any bones broke?" After a fine inspection, the verdict was pronounced. "Nary a one."

It was the best day of my life so far, having may as well come back from the dead. I'd just had the wind knocked out of me and that was all there was to it, but the commotion was every bit worth it. I got to be Linda McCartney three times in a row over it, no questions asked, though nobody would say that was why.

• • •

Leaving these kinds of scenes behind would be the worst crying shame. I didn't want to move off the hill or away from the tree-house or Mrs. Riley or Mrs. Riley's pool. I didn't want to leave the bag swing, even though Dad said he'd hang another in town. I had a feeling he wouldn't, and I'd turn out to be right. Heck, I didn't even want to leave Megen. She had pool toys.

But Dad had heard through the grapevine that he could expect any time now to receive orders for Vietnam, so he'd decided to retire. "I'd survived two wars," he penned in a journal. "I thought it best not to try my luck on a third." And now all our furniture was stacked sky-high and roped to the flatbed of a truck just to move eight blocks to the Ligon house, a stone's throw from the high school. No doubt in my mind, this was all over fifty cents' worth of gas.

There was no denying this was a deluxe house. It had two places to eat—a breakfast room and a dining room—and two places to sit—a den and a living room. You could think to yourself, *What couch should I sit on right now?* and you could just go sit on it. We never said "living room" because Mom called it the music room from the start. It was divided from the den by a set of French doors with sheer white curtains hanging over the glass and had another set that faced the front yard. This was the special room where Wayne's piano stood. Everybody knew it was Wayne's piano even though the rest of us knew our way around the keys. Mom made all of us kids take lessons, but none of us were the natural he was. I didn't hit a single wrong note of "When I Survey the Wondrous Cross" at my recital and, considering the B-flats, that should've said something, but it wasn't easy practicing with a colored-chalk portrait of Wayne over the piano. I didn't blame him for it because I liked him so much, and he couldn't help that he was a genius.

Wayne was already the rehearsal pianist for *The Sound of Music* by the time he was twelve. Lord-a-mercy, there was no keeping a body that talented backstage. His first out-front role in the Arkadelphia community theater was as the cadaver in *Arsenic and Old Lace*, and he did so fine a job playing dead that he made the River City boys' band in *Music Man*. After that, he was the Artful Dodger in *Oliver!*; the crown prince in *The King and I*; Mordred in *Camelot*; Barnaby Tucker in *Hello, Dolly!*; and Junior Babcock in *Mame*. People were all the time saying about Wayne, "Reckon what he'll become?" and "Famous, that's what." They were right to say it, too.

Eventually, Mother set a music stand in front of a chair to the right of the piano where Wayne could set his sheet music and practice the French horn he'd added to his repertoire.

What removed any doubt of his talent at all was how Wayne took high school French and sounded just like he'd been to Paris. Gay was second in talent to Wayne, and soon she'd take French, too. It didn't matter that we couldn't understand a single word they were saying because we were under their spell. There was no telling what Nanny or Pappaw thought about how far we'd come in life, being from the bowels of Arkansas, now that we'd gone French.

• • •

With the move to Twelfth Street came my official promotion in family status: I got to move into a room with my big sister, Gay. This was a groundbreaking shift, a clear acknowledgment that I, a full seven going on eight, had come into girlhood, a needed boost for me since Gay was about to get to wear a bra. This way the future was bright for both of us.

Gay and I had managed to land a whole wing of the house by ourselves next to the driveway, though we would not realize the full potential of our distance from Mom and Dad's and Nanny's rooms until Gay's legs grew long enough to reach from the driver's seat to the pedal.

During the day, I basked proudly and loudly in the new rooming arrangements, but the nights took some getting used to. The mattress wasn't the same on the bed Gay and I now shared and nowhere near as warm. And, frankly, we were so far from everyone else, a kidnapper could have us in Fayetteville by breakfast. I kept these concerns to myself for fear of losing what social progress I'd gained in the eyes of my family members.

Out on the hill, Sandra and Gay had shared a room. Mom and Dad also shared a room with a crib in the corner for Tony. Once Tony could crawl in and out of the crib at will, he volleyed between Wayne's room and our parents' room, depending on a sophisticated teenage boy's tolerance level for a rowdy toddler. These arrangements had left one last bedroom for one final pair: Nanny and me.

In our family, sharing a room equaled sharing a bed. Most of our bed frames and headboards first belonged to other close kin, usually Greens or Rountrees. The same was true for our chests of drawers and end tables. We didn't have much new-bought furniture, and I can't think of a single bed we hadn't inherited. For instance, any one of us or our cousins might end up with Dead-Mammaw's bed and if so, likely where she'd succumbed. These were things we expected. The idea that mattresses should be retired at some reasonable point hadn't occurred to the general population.

All this is to explain how Nanny and I ended up sleeping together on her and Granddaddy Micajah's feather mattress that looked suspiciously like an oversized pillow. There was no actual organization to the stuffing. No buttons, seams, or springs, and no stitching, except on the edges. This meant you were not in control of your mattress. Your mattress was in control of you. When you got ready for bed, you heaved yourself upon it and sunk until it swallowed you whole. Make no mistake, this could be a heavenly respite from the day's evils—unless there was a widely uneven weight distribution between occupants.

By normal practice, I climbed in the bed before Nanny. And by *climbed*, I mean to paint the picture that this bed, like most of its contemporaries, reached halfway to the low ceiling. Having scaled the knoll, I'd curl up on the edge, my eyes droopy, and try to stay awake until Nanny finished her evening toilette. This entailed the usual things like brushing her teeth, soaking her partials, changing from her day dress to her nightgown (Nanny never once wore pants), and setting a mason jar of ice water on her bedside table that would bead up and sweat through the night, drawing the same circle deeper in the varnish.

I always faced away from her and pretended I was asleep to give Nanny privacy, because you weren't to just flit about in front of everybody in your gowntail. I also found it more difficult to sleep if I saw her underpants. I loved Nanny gobs more than I loved Pappaw, but I'd rather stare at his lost eye for a solid minute. I'd never seen any underpants like Nanny's before, nor have I since. They were shaped like Dad's undershorts, big and roomy, with four- or five-inch legs, only they were beige nylon like a woman's slip. This seemed untoward to me, which is why I mostly kept my back to her at changing time.

When I could tell from a series of short grunts that Nanny was in the preliminary stages of launching onto the bed, I'd gather up what mattress I could fit in my fingers and hold on with both hands. Hers was a dramatic entrance. Once the bed stopped quaking, I'd fall asleep, and, naturally, my grip on the mattress would loosen. Then, lost in slumber's sweet bliss, I'd gradually roll down duck hill, sleeping safe and sound in the cleft of the rock.

Sometimes we made it through the night without Nanny having to use the Folgers can. She kept it right in the room with us. I never once asked about this practice nor thought ill of her, but I did calculate that by the time she situated herself just right over the can so as to aim as a woman is disadvantaged to do, she could have twice coursed the fifteen-foot distance down the hall to the bathroom. I concluded that the practice was a perfectly reasonable way to avoid walking the house in the middle of the night and waking the baby, whoever the baby was at the time. Nanny had moved in with Mom and Dad before the signature on their marriage license could dry. They'd earned such a reward, I have to believe, for shaming her with an elopement. With Nanny's seven children and their five, she'd lived with a dozen babies over the years. So if anyone knew how to keep from waking babies, it was Nanny.

Come morning, my mother would often ask my grandmother, "Momma, how'd you sleep last night?"

"Purt near well, I guess," she'd report. "That Bethie's the aw-fullest thing about wantin' to sleep right on your person, though."

With our move into town, Nanny got her own room, and I acquired a new bedmate and a later-model mattress that wasn't fifty pounds of bird feathers sewn up loose in a sheet. I didn't sleep on the small of Gay's back nearly as much as I had Nanny's, and had I, her patience would have understandably run thin. It was time for growing up. But this sudden sleeping independence was no small adjustment. It was scary over there on my side.

● ● ●

During the daytime, I play with Gay's makeup and try on her shoes. She won't care. If she is outside with her friend Robin, I read the folded notes hidden not-too-good in her pajama drawer. All of them are written on notebook paper with smudgy number-two pencils. I can't say anything to Gay on account of how she'd know I'd been into her notes again but her friends orta think of using pencil sharpeners once in a while and they wouldn't make such a mess.

I move from Gay's pajama drawer to her macramé purse and find a tampon with a torn wrapper and study it. I find loose change in the bottom corners with the potato-chip crumbs, but

I don't take it. I'd never take it. I just count it. The lunch tokens don't count as real money, even though they look like quarters. They only count in the school cafeteria. I pull out two torn ticket stubs from football games.

I have a great idea. I'll dig thumbtacks out of that one kitchen drawer and tack the stubs right on our bedroom wall, and I might even find me a blue streamer to hang between them. All this is just right, being as the Arkadelphia High School Mighty Badgers football team is on what everybody in town's calling a winnin' streak. Lordy, we put those Malvern Leopards to shame.

If Gay walks in and catches me in her purse, she'll act mad, but she won't be. She won't holler or anything. I like daytime in the room I share with Gay. It's at bedtime I get butterflies in my stomach. At bedtime I wish I still slept with Nanny. Because on the other side of bedtime comes the Shadow, breaking into my dreams like a burglar with a house key.

The dream is always the same.

I'm in my same house. In my same room. In our same bed. But the shapes and sizes are all wrong. The doors and windows are enormous, like in a giant's room. The ticket stubs on the wall look like big puzzle pieces now, spinning round and round the tacks. Gay is in the same bed with me. I reach out my arm and twinkle my fingertips to touch her sleeve, but she's too far for me to reach. No one is home but us. *Where does everyone go?*

I hear something down the long corridor, a faraway door opening. I don't know how I hear the hinge squeak or why those closer to it can't hear it, but they don't.

There's the sound again. A thumping. Maybe it's my heart. *Shhhh. Listen, listen. Which way is it going?* Sometimes the Shadow turns. Not this time. My heart quickens.

I can hear the creaking of the wooden floor in the hall. The thumping is getting louder, closer. The Shadow is just on the other side of our door now. The doorknob turns slowly, the spindle whines, and the latch retracts. The air in the room changes.

I feel Gay stiffen next to me. I wonder if she feels it, too. I pull the covers up to my nose. *It's a dream, it's just a dream. Go away, Shadow. You are a big knot of terrible bad thoughts. That's all you are. A knot of terrible bad thoughts.*

The room is dark—the spackled ceiling flat now, moonless, starless—but it's a thin kind of dark I can wave my arm through, walk through, find my way through, tear through.

The Shadow is not like that. The Shadow is a dense darkness. Thick. Stuffed. It doesn't speak. It breathes. It wheezes. Its nose whistles.

It draws closer now. Blacker now. Thicker now. It's hovering now. It moves over our bed like the world's blackest cloud. I pull the covers up higher. *I want my mom . . . I want my nanny . . . I want my Wayne.*

I hear the clock on the mantel strike the hour. It's midnight. I hold my breath. Maybe if the Shadow thinks I'm already dead, he'll leave. Trembling, I lower the covers just enough to steal a peek. There it is. The Shadow. Hovering. Wheezing. My eyes widen in terror. The Shadow draws closer. That's when I see it. Plain as the nose on my face. A single strike of lightning on its head. I take a quick breath and squeeze my eyes shut . . . *waiting for the thunder.*

CHAPTER THREE

WHAT WE GREENS LOST in free seats to Ouachita football games when we left the hill, we made up for in free admission to the movies. I don't care who says different, Arkadelphia did not have a hotter spot year-round than the Royal Theater. Name any weekend and as many as twenty people might be lined up at the ticket booth for the seven o'clock. With our flair for the dramatic, our family took to movie theater life like Elvis Presley took to Ann-Margret.

The Royal Theater was the pearl of Main Street. Fuller Drugstore across the street was its solitary competition and only because it had a soda fountain that served root beer floats and said so in white paint on the window. The other businesses on Main—Sterling's five-and-dime, the Dew-Orr Department Store, and Tom Chandler's Shoes, for instance, the latter of which declared itself *America's finest footwear*—had common glass fronts, one no different than the other, and names overhead in plain fonts. These were not eyesores, just nothing special. (The one exception might have been Sterling's, since Sandra had worked there for fifty cents an hour on Saturdays when she was in high school. The way I saw it, this hire had been good for their reputation. Nobody could say she wasn't popular. No telling how it had gone downhill since she'd married.)

The theater was the opposite of "nothing special." It was signature art deco with the word *Royal* in giant cursive letters on the second story accenting a double marquee where, if Dad had enough letters, the titles were spelled right. He ran short on *K*s, but the problem was readily solved when he took a pair of scissors and cut the tops off two *R*s. Improvising was Dad's specialty, and it showed. The triangular space beneath the marquee allowed room for moviegoers to line up at the booth without clogging up the sidewalk. On most days, customers could find Agnes Cox behind the glass, propped on a stool, taking money and sliding tickets through a half-circle opening. No one could accuse her of being young, but folks couldn't hold it against her since it was plain to see she went to Cathryn's House of Beauty every week. Prize in hand, privileged customers entered a set of double doors with small round windows that added a certain showboat mystique. Mr. Brantley, a silver-haired man with a slight build and gentle demeanor, tore tickets and welcomed patrons behind the red velvet cord with a sweep of his right hand. Nothing at all was run-of-the-mill about the Royal Theater. It was Arkadelphia's main event, where dreams were sold and stars were seen.

For seventy cents apiece, anyone was welcome. Whites were welcome to take the official entrance with the doorman and sit downstairs in the main auditorium, and Blacks were welcome to enter a separate door with no doorman at all and buy their tickets and treats at the back of concessions, then follow the Colored signs and climb a set of narrow stairs to the balcony.

Ten years had passed since the Supreme Court declared segregation in public schools to be unconstitutional, but Arkansas, generally speaking, was a bit slow-footed. The molasses at the ankles thickened considerably several years after the ruling when, in 1957, Governor Faubus summoned the Arkansas National Guard to block Black students from the doors of Little Rock's Central High on the first day of school. Arkadelphia was sixty-nine miles downwind and the forecast was relentlessly windy. By 1970, Arkadelphia public schools would fully integrate. But our time at the Royal began in the midsixties, when the shadows of Black and white children together on a playground barely touched.

I was in the lobby when one of the three Black children in my class at school entered the Royal with her family. I looked at her and she looked at me, each with recognition, but not knowing what to do from there, we quickly looked away. I studied the candy selection under the glass like I didn't know every piece by heart. I didn't peek back at my classmate until she and her family filed up the steep stairs, decked in Sunday best, her with white eyelet socks folded above shiny Mary Janes.

Clunky, thick-soled corrective shoes weighed heavy on my feet. I'd still have to wear those awful saddle oxfords another year on account of my bad case of pigeon toes wasn't quite cleared up. "That right foot's still a-turnin' innerd, Letha," Nanny would say, purt near staring a hole through my big toes. "Ain't gonna do that young'un a bit'a good rushin' her outta them shoes."

Mom let me wear Mary Janes on special occasions, like Christmas and Easter, or on a rare Sunday here and there when Gay and I had new matching dresses, fresh off Nanny's sewing machine. Don't imagine I didn't show those shoes off real good. Oh, I did. I sat tall as I could, sticking my feet straight out in front of me, clicking the tips together. I bet the girl from my class was upstairs that very moment clicking hers. Bet she liked the way the patent leather stuck together just a tad, too, like they'd been polished with some Elmer's glue.

Fancy shoes ought not be hid, seemed to me. Families ought not be hid. Folks ought not be hid. Oftentimes nobody has to say something is wrong for a child to know it. I could feel the shame in my chest. It's just that people can have a strange way of outgrowing what they once knew.

Every now and then, when the theater was nearly empty and no one was looking, I'd sneak up the stairs and sit, wondering what the movies looked like from there. There was no pretending the upstairs was kept as nice as the downstairs. The seats were old and stained and the floor sooty. I'd turn my face up and stare at the tubular beam of light coming from the projector in the curious inner sanctum behind the balcony, mesmerized by dust particles afloat like tiny feathers. Sometimes I'd sit in this seat, sometimes that, and tilt my head and squint my eyes toward the screen.

"Well, they can see pretty good." Always *they*. That's the way it was. We soothed our wounded consciences the best we could.

My siblings probably stole up those stairs and wondered similar things, but we wouldn't have told each other. Didn't make any difference anyway. There are some things all the sitting in the world in someone else's seat can't tell you. You'd have to sit in the same skin.

Multiple screens were still figments of wild imaginations. The Royal was a typical one-screen, running a single movie anywhere from two days on, depending on how it was faring at the box office. *Lawrence of Arabia* stayed a whole week and most of the musicals did, too. *Mary Poppins* stayed till Sterling's all but ran out of umbrellas. The long-running hits were how my siblings and I knew movie scripts like real actors, one step removed. We'd carry on during the sad parts like we'd never seen them. I bawled and blew my nose in the girls' restroom for fifteen minutes after *Romeo and Juliet*. Who'd ever seen such a tragedy? In my mind it was me and the boy I liked best at elementary school up on that screen, faint with love, and he hated awful bad to see me go. I stared at him in class come Monday, thinking how he was just fidgeting at his desk, making paper airplanes, like we hadn't died together.

Dad must have been a good soldier, the way he'd won a stack of medals and stayed in the Army so long, but I can't think he ever did anything in his life, first to last, as well as he made popcorn. He could pop every kernel without burning a one and with three simple ingredients: fresh quality corn (don't imagine he didn't know the difference), enough coconut oil to generously bathe the bottom of the aluminum kettle, and a thick blanket of powder-fine, butter-flavored salt. Search the world over and nothing, I'll declare to the death, smells better than movie popcorn just beginning to crack open the hinged lid and spill onto the stainless-steel deck. Dad would turn the pan over at precisely the right second and empty it, while folks stood at the concession stand with mouths agape and glands watering. Then, while the popcorn was nice and hot and as yellow as a bed of daffodils, he'd take his butter-flavored-salt shaker and finish it off with a good dusting.

This exhibition was good business, not only because Dad sold buckets and buckets of popcorn but also because the salt made people thirsty and sent them right back to the counter for soft drinks. All of us kids liked to work when we were at the Royal, as long as we could dart in and out. Wayne was the only one old enough to work real hours and get paid actual money, but this was fair since nobody else got a bad scar from the hot popper. Mr. Brantley had the patience of Job and he'd let Tony tear tickets with him, if for no other reason than to keep him from being a Green Bay Packer and running full steam into the legs of customers. He could bring grown men to their knees playing Bart Starr. Gay and I, on the other hand, worked in the concession stand with mature sophistication, and no job ever had better perks. We could drink all the coke and eat all the popcorn we wanted as long as we used a Dixie cup and a pickle bag.

Now, in those days and in our region every soda pop was called a coke. To misunderstand the meaning was to waste considerable product, and Dad wasn't fond of waste. The process went like this.

We'd say, "May I have your order, please?" Mom taught us, "Never *can I*, always *may I*." It was better manners, she insisted, and we didn't want Nanny to say, "Them young'uns ain't got manner one."

The customers would then say, "Let's see," pausing for what felt like five minutes and tapping their chins like we'd gotten new choices since they were here last week. Finally, they'd say some variation of, "I'll have a Snickers, a dill pickle, a medium popcorn, and a large coke."

This is when we'd say, "What kind of coke?" And they'd specify.

Orange coke.

Grape coke.

Sprite coke.

Dr. Pepper coke.

If you wanted a Coca-Cola, you had to say so. On occasion someone ordered *a suicide*, meaning living on the edge with a shot of every kind of soda in one cup. The only beverage we kept out of the suicide was pickle juice. That wasn't considered a coke on account of it being a juice. It had to be ordered separately and only while supplies lasted. We'd pour it straight out of the pickle jar—yellow-green with a few stray seeds—into a cup of crushed ice. If we said, "May I serve you a pickle with it?" I could bet a dime and two nickels they'd say, "No, just the juice." "Why not?" I'd want to ask, but I knew the answer. They hated pickles.

Having taken the order, we'd then say, "Comin' right up" as cheerful as you please and we'd get busy. The first year Dad ran the Royal, my forehead barely reached the counter and I'd have to stand on my tiptoes to push the rim of the cup against the fountain lever. The only way I could know if the cup was full was to let it overflow. The customers didn't seem to mind. They'd just snatch extra napkins from the silver container—*one-two-three* brisk-like—and dry off the cup, leaving the damp wads right on the glass counter. I'd thank them, and then, if the wads weren't too wet, I'd use them to dry off the underside of my arm and my armpit.

The job all of us liked the least was cleaning up the auditorium between movie showings. If we had the foresight, this was prime time to shoot out the door and across the street to the five-and-dime to admire the toys. You wouldn't believe how people would knock over their cokes, spill their popcorn, and throw their candy wrappers on the floor and just leave it all there like they didn't have manner one. Every pair of shoes we owned had two or three flattened kernels stuck to the bottoms, still daffodil yellow. Monday through Friday, 8:30 to 3:30, our shoes stuck to the floor when we got up from our desks, making crackling sounds the whole class could hear.

All us kids except Sandra came of age at the Royal Theater doing things we ought not to have done and right under our dad's nose. Wayne was first. He told me himself how he came into manhood.

"It was right there on the back row of the center section during a matinee showing of *Rome Adventure*," he told me later. "I waited for a dark moment."

My eyes widened, knowing just how certain scenes could make the auditorium feel like nighttime.

"My heart was thumping," he said.

Mine was, too.

"Then there it was."

"There *what* was?" I asked, on pins and needles.

"Troy Donahue and Suzanne Pleshette were on a Vespa, speeding off to parts unknown, and disappeared through a tunnel."

I pictured the scene like I was there. "Then what?"

That's when he said it straight out. "I jumped on the opportunity and laid a big kiss right on Belinda Bippus's pillowy lips."

Things like Belinda Bippus's pillowy lips were why the pluses of hanging out at the Royal outweighed the minuses by a country mile, unless a kid ate too many treats and threw up in the aisle. Best you could do was hope it was Tootsie Dots. If it was a hot dog, there was almost no recovering.

The goods, however, belonged to those of us with a keen eye. We knew who'd come with who, who was dating who, who'd broken up with who, who put his arm around who, and whose mom snuck in late and sat in the back and was about to catch who and who. And that's not all. If we happened by the lobby on the weekend of a naughtier movie, we knew who'd bought a ticket on Saturday night and sat in church on Sunday morning like they hadn't.

CHAPTER FOUR

I COULD EXIT THE ROYAL THEATER with a pickle bag full of popcorn, take an immediate left on the sidewalk of Main, a quick right on North Seventh after looking both ways, make a beeline down a few blocks and, before I got down to the kernels, enter the doors of a place homier to me than the red-brick Tudor on Twelfth would ever be. School aside, the only place I spent more time than the Royal Theater was First Baptist Church of Arkadelphia. The building was nothing less than palatial, bouncing off the pupils of a child's wide eyes. The traditional tan-brick structure stood erect, several stories high, with tall, slender stained-glass windows encasing a sanctuary meant to be taken seriously. Wings to the right and left held scads of educational space, a fine church library, a spacious preschool department and nursery, and, on the bottom floor, a full church kitchen adjoining the fellowship hall. Big as it was to a small child, I knew every square inch of it, save the boys' restroom. We who were raised in those halls in those days roamed and ran them freely.

When it came to sophistication, we were right up there with the Presbyterians. We were walking distance from Ouachita Baptist University, whose students were required to attend church, and lucky for us only a handful of them had cars. Jesus walked everywhere he went and they could, too. Some impressive Ouachita professors also graced our halls and warmed our pews, including those from a music department of fine repute. These often sang our solos and fed and led our choirs.

We Greens were not overzealous with religious talk at home. Zeal within our walls was reserved primarily for good manners, saying *yessir* and *no sir*, *yes ma'am* and *no ma'am*, and *may I be excused* when we were done eating supper. But rain or shine, sleet or snow, we were taken to church no less than two and a half hours three times a week—Sunday mornings, Sunday evenings, and Wednesdays right after school and all evening. Tossed like softballs nearly fresh from the womb to church nursery workers, we never knew anything different. They may as well have been midwives standing in the delivery rooms with our mother.

In those days, churches didn't have a robust theology of germs. We were exposed to every possible malady as early as possible. As kids, if we had colds: "Here's you a handkerchief. Blow hard, wipe good, and I'll be by to get you in a few hours." If we had what my people called the bowel complaint: "Don't wait too long to get to the bathroom. Blow hard, wipe good, and I'll be by to get you in a few hours." That's just how it was. No amount of whining was going to change it.

But I think all the time, what if something *had* changed it?

What if I'd whined my way out of spending what seemed half my young life within those walls?

My church believed in doing stuff in front of people. That could mean showing off with five-dollar words only a few knew, or singing loud enough to be heard from ten pews away, or never looking at a hymnal even for third and fourth verses, or sitting spit-distance from the pulpit every single service, or laying a check faceup in the offering plate, or looking badly pained while playing the organ during the offertory. These we practiced on a regular basis. But there were other times at our church when doing stuff in front of people was a way to let them know you'd made a big decision. Sometimes it wasn't until we made it public to our congregation that we knew just how big a decision it was. The first time this happened to me, I was nine years old.

I slid my hand down the wooden rail of the small pool behind the choir loft and stuck the tip of my toes in the water and wiggled them. I was scared it would be cold even though I was told different. It wasn't hot like a bath, but it wasn't freezing like the swimming pool on the first day of summer break either.

"Go ahead, honey," whispered the woman who was in charge of helping the girls and ladies get their white robes on, her hand gently patting my back. Mom had dropped me off with her a half hour earlier, giving me a quick reassuring squeeze then hurrying out the door so she could sit with the rest of our family in the sanctuary. I don't recall the lady's name, but I remember her comfortable way as she helped me out of my Sunday dress and my slip. I wrapped my arms around my bare tummy, glad I got to keep on my unders. Anyway, she didn't seem creepy or scary or like she really even noticed my belly button was an outie.

"You'll wear the ones you have on right into the water," Mom had said. "I put another pair in this little sack." I nodded as she handed it to me. I decided to imagine myself wearing swimsuit bottoms. A swimsuit would have been a good idea. Somebody should have thought of that because what if Mom had dropped the paper sack in the hall? And what if she'd put my name on the tag of the unders with a black marker like at summer camp? How was I supposed to recover from one of the Neel boys picking up that sack?

The woman chatted softly as she pulled the robe down over my head and I stuck my arms through the sleeves. "You doing okay, sweetie?"

"Yes, ma'am."

"Today's a big day."

I nodded.

"You'll get to take home a New Testament from the church. Isn't that something?"

"Yes, ma'am."

Brother Reeves—that's what we called our preacher—was standing waist-deep in the water where everyone could see him. He was addressing the congregation while an older kid, drenched and dripping from head to toe, was climbing the short set of stairs to the boys' side. The pool stirred with his retreat, and small waves broke against the glass front of the baptismal. Brother Reeves was finishing up what he'd been saying and was now reaching toward me with his left hand, twinkling the tips of his fingers just like I was twinkling the tips of my toes.

I put my right foot down on the first step, my left on the second, still holding tight to the rail. I took a quick glimpse beyond the glass and saw choir members in their robes and stoles, necks craned to face us. There was Peggy Horton, a high soprano. She did the special music at our church on a regular basis and her name would be in the bulletin just like this: *Special Music: Peggy Horton.*

Brother Reeves was always in the bulletin, too, under *Sermon* but never as Brother Reeves. In writing he was always *Dr. Sam Reeves*. I didn't know whose doctor he was. He wasn't ours. We saw Dr. Ross when we were sick. He came right to the house. I don't believe Dr. Reeves had once been to our house in town nor had he ever looked in our ears. This is not to say I didn't like him. I did. I just didn't know if he was a fit doctor. He was a fit preacher, though, the way he stood tall at the pulpit like his mother raised him for it and used important words and knew when to get loud and when to get quiet according to how sleepy we were getting. He also usually ended on time, which was how my family calculated who was called to preach and who wasn't.

I took the third step and reached out my hand, returning Brother Reeves's twinkle fingers. I couldn't see the congregation, but I wondered if they were standing or sitting. I hoped they were sitting because of Nanny.

"Looks to me like them folks could make up their mind," Nanny would say, "whether they want us a-settin' or standin'." Nanny should not be blamed for feeling this way. She and all her friends from Sunday school who sat together during the worship service were as old as Moses and just as white-haired, only they wore hats and he didn't. By the time they'd help each other to their feet, weaving and wobbling and rattling the pew, the rest of us were breaking into the third verse of "Blessed Assurance": *Perfect submission, all is at rest. I in my Savior am happy and blest.* "I'm plum worn out by 'Blest Be the Tie.'" That was the song we sang at the very end of the service, all standing and holding hands.

Indeed all were not at rest nor happy and blest if you asked Nanny. But I couldn't do anything about it, up there in the baptistry with Brother Reeves, him in a white gown with bare feet and no more a doctor than I was. He had my hand now and gently tugged me toward the center of the small pool. His familiar face widened with a smile. The water was dense against me, slow-moving like honey, its warmth creeping up the fabric on my back. As he steered me directly in front of him, I rehearsed the instructions in my mind one last time, slipping my feet under a small bar on the baptismal floor. This feature was supposed to keep me from turning a backward flip when the time came, but I didn't know if the plan was going to work. I felt like it was made for bigger feet than mine. From the space I was detecting between my feet and the bar, I was pretty sure that if Brother Reeves got too enthusiastic, even a grown man was at risk of flipping. I curled both sets of toes up around the bar as tight as I could, then cupped my hands over my nose and mouth the way they'd said to do.

Brother Reeves put one hand steady between my shoulder blades and the other one up in the air like he was waving at Mrs. Reeves. "In obedience to the command of our Lord and Savior Jesus Christ and upon your profession of faith, I now baptize you, my sister, Beth Green, in the name of the Father and of the Son and of the Holy Spirit, for the forgiveness of your sins . . ."

He said other words, too, but I missed them. For one thing, I got distracted by Brother Reeves calling me his sister. I needed to think on that a minute. Second thing, even though this is what I'd come for, I was still a good bit surprised by the swiftness of the dunking. Whatever God does during a water baptism, I hoped he was paying attention right then or he'd have missed his opportunity. Brother Reeves, who was usually inclined toward slow motion, threw his waving hand over my nose, bent me backward, stuck my whole head under water, then swung me up in a whiplash. There was no *ready, set, go*. There was no *on the count of three*. In two seconds flat, I'd been buried with Christ in baptism and raised—and I do mean raised in every way since my feet had instantly come out from under the bar—to walk in newness of life. I could tell you this much about the First Baptist Church of Arkadelphia: there was no changing your mind once you got in that water with Brother Reeves. He was coming for your nose and you were going under. This was just as well. I didn't want to change my mind anyway.

They said I wouldn't get water in my nose, but yes, I did, and I figure I swallowed some of it, too, and they may as well have allowed it since they caused it. I was baptized inside and outside, through and through, and in my nose and down my throat. My baptism was in my stomach, in my arms, and in my legs. That's how I was sure it took and that I never needed another one as long as I lived. I didn't know how Brother Reeves could see with a spray of droplets on his bifocals, but apparently he could, since he steered me by the hand back to those same steps where the woman in charge of baptized girls was waiting for me with a white towel. By the look on her face, I must have done just fine. I could hear the curtain closing over the baptistry, and I guessed Peggy Horton was heading to the microphone for special music, giving Brother Reeves time to get back in his church clothes over there on the boys' side.

I was shaking by now, cold from the air-conditioning hitting my sopped skin, but I was content. I'd done what my grandparents and parents and my brother and sisters before me had done, and I was soaked to the bone to prove it. In no time at all, Mom was there to get me. She finished drying me off and got me redressed and combed my hair in a hurry so we could go back into the service. You didn't get to miss the sermon just because you got baptized. You didn't even get a snack. You just got a New Testament.

Mom and I tiptoed into the service from the back while the ushers were passing the offering plate. What would normally be rude, like wet hair at church, was perfectly fine for people who'd just been baptized. You were allowed to do almost anything, and everybody would just look at you and smile. You could step on their feet all you wanted getting down the pew. Mom and I made it to our usual row and scooted in with our people. As I settled in next to Gay, I could see Nanny tucked amid her friends further down the row, her big King James in her lap. Pretty soon she leaned forward just enough for me to see through the pale blue net of her pillbox hat that she was happy. I fought a grin and squeezed strands of hair between two fingers, dripping water on page 204 of the Baptist hymnal, "Nothing but the Blood."

I couldn't concentrate on the sermon that day. My gaze flew like a butterfly in spring around the sanctuary, landing on the shoulder of this person and that. In an end seat of the loft sat Mrs. Shambarger, my church choir teacher. By the time I'd turn twelve, she would also be my handbell teacher, assigning me F, F-sharp, and G. I'd be decent at them, too. In the side section and several rows up, I could see the back of Mrs. Mary King's head. I'd have known Mrs. King's head anywhere, so I lowered my wings and landed there for a good while. Nobody at First Baptist Church was more familiar to me than she was. She taught missions classes for girls every Wednesday night, and she kept moving up with my age group. I never knew if she kept promoting with us because she loved us or to spare another teacher the grief, but it seemed to me she wouldn't have us over for slumber parties if she didn't like us. We'd spend the night on her den floor with our pillows and pallets more times than we could count, and she'd always fix a foreign food so we could talk about missionaries in that country. She had two wiener dogs that were a little heavy on their feet, I guessed from us dropping them our foreign foods.

Scattered all over the sanctuary were kids and grown-ups we

ate alongside every week at Wednesday night supper in the fellowship hall. Same people and, most of the time, the same menu: a pale slice of ham, a scoop of green beans, one split roll, one pat of margarine, and one red cinnamon apple ring arranged on heavy white plates in our church kitchen by fast-moving women.

I couldn't see where Mrs. Lizzie, a little sparrow of a woman, was perched in the sanctuary, but I'd already seen her flitting about our department that morning anyway. She was my Sunday school teacher and had the same luck getting our class to pay attention as Mrs. King did. I don't know why she never told us to quit trading arm tickles. I feel like we might have stopped if she'd scared the living daylights out of us occasionally, but she had other fine qualities to make up for failing at fussing. She always had extra Sunday school quarterlies because hardly any of us could find ours at home. She knew all our families and could recall our prayer requests from last week about things like how the cat had coughed up a hair ball on the chenille bedspread. She hadn't done a bit of good about our lying and cheating, though. We'd still check off *Read Sunday school lesson* and *Read Bible daily* on the attendance sheet every week, like it was fine to sin at church.

These were the people, and these were the things, my wandering mind had landed on that Sunday during the sermon with my wet hair when I heard a disembodied voice coming from somewhere in the back of the sanctuary giving Brother Reeves a loud throaty *a-a-a-a-men*. I never knew what old man the voice belonged to, but it came like clockwork every week, midsermon then again at the end. Not many people at First Baptist could talk during church service without getting in trouble. Luckily this was the amen signaling the sermon's end, and we were standing to our feet, turning to the hymn of invitation. That week it was page 363, "I Surrender All." It usually was.

This was the point in the service that Brother Reeves would ask the congregation if we'd turned from our sins and accepted Jesus and been born again, and if you hadn't and wanted to, you were invited to walk the aisle straight to him and tell him so. He made it easy, too, stepping down from the platform to floor level.

No one wanted to turn from their sins that particular day. I always felt sorry for Brother Reeves when no one wanted to turn from their sins. Several weeks earlier I'd wanted to, though, the best I knew how and the best I'd sinned. I'd told my mom I was ready to join the church just like the rest of the Greens besides Tony, just seven after all, and that I wanted to take the Lord's Supper next round. She'd asked me a few questions. Had I accepted Jesus as my personal Savior? Well, yes, I had. Well, when then? I couldn't pinpoint the precise moment, but I knew I had.

I'd believed my preschool Sunday school teachers when they held up those posters and told stories about how Jesus could call tiny men down from trees and make the leopards clean and cause the blind to see. We sat there and heard every third word in a circle of baby-bear-size chairs, drinking orange Hi-C and twirling Nabisco butter cookies on our fingers. I'd believed my Sunday school teachers again in first grade, and second and third, when they told us about how Jesus died and rose again so we could be forgiven and live with God forever. Now, I didn't know much about heaven, but I knew from the way Brother Reeves scowled when he threatened sinners with the bad place that heaven was the better of the two. Mom said I could walk the aisle next Sunday.

Brother Reeves always had those who'd come forward stay in the front of the sanctuary after the closing prayer so the congregation could line up and give them "the right hand of fellowship." Gay and I would snicker in line and dare each other to offer our left hand instead, but we lost the courage when it came time. When I walked the aisle myself, little kids and teenagers and grown-ups as far as eye could see came to shake my hand and the hands of others who'd come. Old folks with bodies bent over canes shuffled forward and reached out bony hands speckled with purple spots and striped with inky veins.

"How wonderful," this and that one would say.

"Welcome to the family!"

"I worked in the nursery when you were two," one lady said.

"Congratulations, young lady," scads of people said.

I did fine at first, then something came over me. A knot the size of a kid's fist clogged my throat and refused to be swallowed. My lip started quivering, and tears began rolling down my cheeks in Caddo rivers. This did nothing to stop the line. People acted like it was normal and just kept coming. I received their fellowship with my right hand and tried to hide my face and dry my tears with my left forearm.

I knew from the faces, words, and handshakes of those who'd long since made the same decision and stood in the same spot as me that something more important than I knew was happening. I'd thought to join the church that day and to publicly say I was a Christian. Christ had thought to call me forward that day to start saving my scrawny neck.

That day I walked the aisle, nobody in my family said a word on the way home about how I'd acted a fool and been a crybaby. Nanny just did what she always did. She squirmed in her seat in our VW bus, pulled at her dress and snapped the elastic at her waistline, then said, "Don't nobody get between me and the house when we pull up and I don't mean maybe. This girdle's killing me. Purt near ain't took a breath all mornin'. I reckon it shrunk in the warsher." Momma amened nice and long and low, sounding just like that old man at church and meaning to, funny like she was.

The best days of my young childhood would be lived up and down the heel-scuffed halls of First Baptist Church and in and out the swinging doors of the Royal. But *best* would shortly become a relative term, as it does in every life, and no haven of playfulness would remain unscathed.

CHAPTER FIVE

I'D SEEN IT BEFORE, how the daylight could turn as dark as night and the wind lose its temper, pulling shrubs from the garden and ripping picket fences off a yard, and a whole house could lift swiftly off the ground, sucked into the tail of a furious twister. I'd seen how a house could whirl round and round in a raging storm, the terrified insider clawing for anything holding still. I'd seen how a kid's whole world and the people she knew best could be caught up in the fury, debris flying and heavens roaring like a freight train. Whole trees could be plucked from the ground by their roots, sent hurling through the atmosphere like tumbleweeds. Grown-ups just outside a wide-open window, little more than arms' reach away, deafened to the child's pleas.

Something happens up there in the dark, stormy air that can

turn an average bully pedaling a bike into an ugly witch riding a broom. Minds can go missing in a storm like that. A heart can fly out from under a rib cage. Courage can be ripped away like a sheet off a clothesline.

I'd seen it all splayed on a silver screen, how a house could spin off its slab and enter a vortex of violent imaginations. Then I felt it from within my own walls. I saw it with my own eyes. I reeled to its whirling. I lived it in my own skin, there in our house on Twelfth Street.

Madness came for us. It descended on our roof, spilled over our gutters, and surrounded our house. It seeped through the cracks around our windows. This madness layered our faces, blanketed our bodies, entered our pores, and infected our blood. It haunted our rooms at night like a ghoul. It hammered, then shattered, our security. I was eleven, in the passenger seat of our car coming home from Little Rock, when I'd never again have the luxury of simply wondering if something was wrong. But somewhere, stuffed deep inside a drawer of my mind, I'd always known. A child doesn't pull chunks of her hair and chunks of her memory out of her head over nothing.

Mom told me that morning our plans had changed. Dad was taking me to my regularly scheduled orthodontist appointment to have my braces tightened. Arkadelphia was too small a town for its own orthodontist, so we made the one-hour drive every few weeks. We were house poor and up to our necks in debt, so Dad, understandably, would have preferred to forego the expense, but Mom convinced him of the necessity. "We're not talking about crooked teeth, Al. The child can't close her lips over them."

None of my siblings required braces, but I'd tripped and fallen mouth-first into a coffee table at age six, shoving the top set of my baby teeth into my gums and displacing the permanent teeth above them. My fate was sealed. I could either wear corrective wires for years to come or have the world's worst overbite.

I didn't want Dad to take me by myself. I reminded Mom how they'd both gone every other time. "And after my appointment, we go lickety-split to Casa Bonita, all three of us, so I can eat before my teeth get sore, remember, Mom? Then we head straight home so you can be here when Tony and Gay get out of school. It always works, doesn't it, Mom? We're always back on time."

"I know, I know," she said.

I kept insisting we could manage it. "And Nanny's here anyway if we're a few minutes late. But we won't be, I promise. We don't even have to go out to eat."

"Aw," she said. "Aren't you sweet." She wished she could go, and I knew it was true, but something had come up at one of the schools. She laid out my favorite outfit: a bright-green sleeveless jumper with culottes and big white polka dots. It was sailor style with a square-knot tie at the bottom of the V-neck collar. I'd just gotten my first training bra. I wouldn't start my period for another year.

The drive up to Little Rock, just me and Dad, went fine, mostly because we listened to the radio till it got too staticky. Even then, long as I could tell what song was playing under the pop and crackle, I still knew all the words on account of Gay being a teenager and us sharing a room. Dad got cranky about finding a parking place at the orthodontist's office, but before I could chew my fingernails plumb off like Nanny declared I was going to, me and Dad were in the waiting room. Soon I was lying back in the light-green chair, getting my wires cranked tight as a drum. I liked my orthodontist. He had a lot of good teeth and was always smiley, and this seemed just right to me, him being in the mouth business.

It was on our way home from Little Rock, just after the

buildings and concrete turned to countryside and cows, that my dad switched off the radio and got quiet. We were still getting a signal clear as a whistle on KAAY-AM 1090, so I thought Dad was about to say something. But he didn't.

There's a good kind of quiet that has nothing at all inside it to weigh it down. It's the kind of quiet where a mind is alight with all sorts of thoughts, like what exotic animals your mom might let you keep in your room if you promised to feed them yourself, and wouldn't it be something if cars could fly. But this wasn't that kind of quiet. This was the kind of quiet where the air got thick in the car like I was breathing cotton.

I looked at Dad out of the corner of my eye, trying to decipher what he was concentrating on, the way his jaw was clenching and loosening.

"Come over here and sit next to me," he said, patting the seat, the corner of his mouth twitching up and down unnaturally—grin to frown, grin to frown—him still looking straight ahead like he was right there and somewhere else all at once. I didn't want to scoot over because I liked where I was sitting just fine, but Dad's way was bossing, not asking. He pulled me by my bare arm, tugged at my collar.

No, no, I don't want to. I want to sit by the door. I want my mom. I want my nanny. I want my Wayne. My thoughts screamed but my mouth was stuck shut. The cotton I'd breathed turned to glue. I cried, and he laughed.

Maybe a dad can do a lot of things and a child can think he's still okay in other ways, but not the kind of things my dad did to me. No kind of good dad does what my dad did to me. I knew that, even without knowing names for what he'd done. Names for what he was. He was a no-count dad. Only dad I had. And he was a no-count dad.

• • •

The Ligon house looked different after we got home, like it had shifted ten degrees off the concrete, betraying a crooked roofline. The brick was darker than I'd remembered. I'd thought all along it was red, but I could see now that it wasn't. It was as brown as mud. The light bulbs were dimmer in the lamps on the end tables and in the ceiling fixtures overhead. The filaments were starting to flicker now. The off-white paint on the walls had no white at all.

Maybe a little time went by. In my memory, gale-force winds began to whistle instantly, and pebbles and twigs pecked our windowpanes like hail, but traumatic events have a way of jumbling time. What I know for certain is that no time in a child's upbringing is a good time for her mother to drop out of sight. And no time is worse than when a child's been traumatized by her father and needs her mother to know it. What I also know is that a mother can't always help herself. A hatch opens up under her feet.

Mom took ill. That much is clear to me now. Hindsight can dispel a certain measure of thick haze, but no explanation was ever given at the time to help Gay, Tony, and me process what was happening. Everything became shadows and secrets and tightly shut doors. All we were able to recognize was that our attentive mother, whose children had been her whole world, folded up inside herself, becoming as fragile as papershell for the larger part of four years.

Wayne had gone to college and, with him, our theatrical stage light and the sound of a piano soothing the night. He was in and out of the house through those years and no stranger to the sting of the swarming storm, but even if he'd remained, he couldn't possibly have saved us. He couldn't have saved himself. The madness was bigger than the sum of us. Sandra was many miles away, starting her family. It was the six of us—Dad, Mom, Nanny, Gay, Tony, and me—under a roof that was blowing off in sheets of shingles. Nanny grew increasingly frantic but also old, and her wringing hands were tied. Dad lent himself, practically nothing withholding, to a pitch-black bent. Mom went to bed and left the three of us wide awake and, with a rabid ferocity, a house ajar became a house unhinged.

Mom would emerge for periods of time and seem a lot like her old self. Relieved and overjoyed, we kids would reciprocate and act like our old young selves. *Ask no questions and tell no troubles.* She'd do all the regular tasks and go all the usual places. She'd watch her favorite stories and chirp with her delicious wit. And, for this while, we'd have our mother back, coherent, cooking and washing clothes, but still too fragile around the edges for us to ever settle in and think we'd be all right. Something about the twitching of her eyes and fingertips.

Without any further warning, the sun wouldn't come up the next morning or the next, and we'd swear on a King James we'd never be all right again. She'd do baffling, bone-rattling things like writing a name across a wall or marking a face out of a picture or leaving a nonsensical note or laughing with an unsettling cackle. She placed a phone call to Wayne in a state of hysteria telling him she was ending her life. He sped recklessly through stop signs, ran a light, and jumped curbs to make it in time to intervene. When he bolted into the house, he found Mom sipping coffee, smashing the butt of a cigarette into the bowl of a brown ashtray and blowing its last mouthful of smoke, chin upward, lower lip outward, like nothing ever happened.

We could go days spared of the more unsettling acts, but we had little respite from the black cloud that held Mom hostage, and she had none at all. We would never have answers to many of our questions. We'd never know whether her symptoms were of chronic mental illness alone or exacerbated by the misuse of over-the-counter and prescription drugs. We were so young the latter wouldn't have dawned on us had it not been almost impossible to awaken her at times. She wasn't drinking. We knew that much. The one thing Dad did not allow—the unpardonable sin in his eyes—was alcohol in our home. While this would explain its later appeal to his children, it did not explain our mother's lapses into sleep too deep to stir.

Sometimes Gay, Tony, or I would need something parental that couldn't wait. Maybe it was a required signature on a school document or permission to spend the night with a friend. We'd need a ride to an activity or perhaps just an excuse to make sure she was breathing. We had two parents, but without question, Gay and I trusted our worn and weary sleeping beauty far more than our fully functioning father. We wished to be in no way beholden to him. During the apex of these four mean years, if he happened to be home when Mom was holed up in their room, neither we nor Nanny were allowed access to her.

"Don't touch that door," he'd say, all snarled up like a dog about to bite, if we were tarrying in the hall by their room, us kids wanting our mom and Nanny wanting her girl awful bad.

I wasn't about to give him any back talk, but Nanny would try to reason with him. "Al," she'd say, most uncharacteristically pleading, "that's my daughter in there. I need to check on her."

"I just did!" he'd growl. Then he'd come up with some way to make it sound like leaving Mom alone in that deep, dark hole was in her best interest. "She's sick and needs to sleep!" And that would be the end of it, as long as he was around.

But when he wasn't home, which was often the case, we three kids would brave the deep if we were desperate enough.

This is how it would go: Gay first, me right behind her, my hands on her shoulders, and Tony right behind me, his hands on my shoulders, like a three-car train. We made it a game for Tony's sake. For all our sakes. We'd open the door quietly, and the creaking hinges would set off a familiar repartee.

"Shhhhhhh!"

"I am shushing. You shush your own self."

"Would you shut up?"

"*You* shut up!"

"You're gonna wake her up!"

"We came to wake her up!"

"Well, we're not ready to wake her up!" That much was true, and we all knew it, so we shut up.

We'd let our eyes adjust to the darkness that she maintained with heavy curtains drawn. We'd then move our tiny train—*tiptoes, everybody*—toward the side of the bed with the lump of human clay beneath the covers. Gay was not only the eldest. She was also the bravest. "Mom?" she'd say, then we three would break train and sprint back to the doorway, waiting for her to answer. We knew that when she did, it would come with a startled and disoriented shriek of "What? What? What?" and scare us half to death.

We'd repeat this procedure about four times, increasing the volume, and occasionally getting so tickled we laughed ourselves into three little balls. Laughing was how we coped with the absurdity of living. Sure enough, she'd finally wake up with a shout and sit straight up like a corpse in an open coffin on Alfred Hitchcock, and we'd have the jitters for the next solid hour.

Dad told us Mom was crazy. He'd told her so, too. He claimed she'd lost her mind and was making things up, like how he was up to no good with another woman.

"Well, *are* you?" This was Gay. She'd go eye to eye with him.

Braver than Tarzan. Just one time I saw Dad haul off and slap her right in the face for talking to him that way. Didn't scare her none. She was dog-tired of him about now. I figure he knew she had it in her to slap him back.

"Am I *what*?" he retorted angrily.

"Are you having an affair?" She spit each word out separately, almost like she was banging the heel of a shoe to the linoleum with every syllable.

"Hell, no!" He said it just like that, and he didn't cuss much, him being churchy, so when he did, I knew he was lying like a plump cat on a warm windowsill.

It would take Gay and me weeks to stumble on proof he'd done exactly what he'd said he didn't. He was wrong about Mom. She wasn't crazy. She was caught. Chained in a cell that had become unbearable. And her mind, for a time, suffered a compound fracture as surely as a skull hitting a windshield in a head-on collision. She'd live, but for no short while, she wouldn't wish to.

• • •

One evening when Dad was at work and the rest of us were preoccupied, Mom walked out the front door and vanished into the dusk. Nanny alerted Gay and me, explaining how she'd heard the front door and thought nothing of it, then realized Mom was the only one missing. She'd waited a few minutes, hoping she'd return quickly without incident so Gay and I could be none the wiser. Gay was a licensed driver by now, but her normal enthusiasm to take the wheel was suddenly drenched by an awful apprehension. We phoned Dad at the Royal, told him what had transpired, and begged him to find Mom. He came home "to get the full story," he said, and to wait for her to walk through the door. We didn't talk back to Dad sass-mouth unless we were looking for a fight. But that night we were sufficiently inconsolable to insist he take to the car and search for our mother and Nanny's daughter *and your wife, Dad. Remember her?*

Never once did we step toward the phone in the breakfast room to call the police. We Greens were a well-known family in a small college town. A Christian family, with high visibility at church. Dad was in the Lions Club. He was an officer in the Chamber of Commerce. He was head of his Sunday school department, for crying out loud. Wayne was already legendary in Arkadelphia and he'd barely cracked twenty. Gay was drum majorette of the Arkadelphia High School Badger Marching Band. To our knowledge, no one was onto us yet. I suppose, the way we saw ourselves, we weren't the kind of people who get the police involved. If you asked us, it would have been the kiss of death in that town, no living it down.

It's an oddity how one small detail can melt your heart like wax. With an angst that had gathered the loose skin of her face into a tight knot, Nanny said, "I think Letha was barefooted." No way under heaven would Mom head out the front door without shoes. Not if she were in her right mind. Disgruntled, Dad acquiesced to our urging, our shaming, and left in pursuit of our mom.

Helplessness hollowed our chests of all things hopeful, giving panic a place to pool and roil. We distracted Tony as long as we could. He knew little to nothing about Dad's suspected double life. He knew our family was out of kilter. He knew Mom was often unavailable and seemed unwell, but he was Dad's shadow, often at the Royal and shielded from much that had come to light in our home. The two of them shared a relationship the rest of us hadn't had. Wayne was musical and artistic, a momma's boy. Tony was athletic and rough-and-tumble, a daddy's boy. Gay and

I didn't tinker with that. It kept our little brother less aware and more insulated. Though only a few years older than he, we protected him the best we knew how and kept our mouths shut except for the secrets we told in hushed tones to each other.

Neither Gay, Nanny, nor I sat down for the next hour. We took turns pacing the den floor and standing at the picture window, leaning over the couch, looking for a familiar figure to emerge across the schoolyard. When our panic surpassed what could be hidden from Tony, he entered the mayhem with us. It's an awful thing to watch a knowing that no child should ever have to know take place on a child's face.

"We can't find Mom" is all we said. What else had to be said? When your mom is missing, what else matters?

Tony's infectious smile, adorably crooked, first went flat then flipped upside down like a boot had kicked over a dog's bowl. His lower lip rolled out and quivered. When Tony cried, a most curious thing happened to his eyes. The tears gathered his thick brown lashes into points that made his pupils look like the centers of two twinkling stars. Mom may have been missing, but I guess the way Gay saw it, his big sisters weren't. She took hold of his hand and did not let it go, but neither did she panic one iota less. She dragged him along with her, every compulsive step she took, darting from window to window, from front door to back. He went willingly, apparently feeling safer in it than outside it.

Please, God, please, God, we're begging now. Can you hear us now? Please, Lord.

What I recall with complete clarity in those grueling minutes waiting for some word on Mom is lighting up a cigarette and puffing it like I'd smoked my entire young life. It seemed the thing to do. The thing Mother would have done. She'd left her cigarettes and matchbook at home. *Why would she have done that?*

We heard a car in the driveway and froze. A minute or so later, Dad walked through the back door with Mom, neither of them saying a word. Dazed, Mom walked straight past us and into the kitchen and we heard the kettle clang and the clicking of the stove burner lighting. "Where was she?" Nanny asked Dad, her voice high and feverish, a crumpled tissue in her hand.

"I found her at the river." Sometimes there aren't enough cigarettes.

I'd never see those waters the same way again. They'd been infected with fear now, the gentle lapping at the shore becoming ghostly whispers of *what if, what if, what if, what if.* We were a different kind of river people now.

• • •

I'd transition from junior high to early high school during this protracted season of instability. Every school morning of the ninth grade, I'd take a deep breath, open the front door, walk down the concrete steps, cross Twelfth Street then the schoolyard, consciously trying to drop off the most obvious pieces of my brokenness. They'd be waiting for me like bread crumbs to pick up on the way home, making sure I found the right house with all the right wrongs.

I couldn't have fooled any adult paying attention. I was a strong, successful student suddenly making Ds in two classes. I was a people person no longer able to look people in the eye. I wore grown-up makeup and my skirts too short. I had no shortage of boyfriends but no tools for handling them. I was going places I had no business going with a sister three years older. She reasoned—and she was right—that my going with her was safer than my staying at home without her. I was a good girl doing bad things. I was a bad girl doing good things. I was spiraling in our spinning house, there in the air where witches fly.

The only thing that terrified me more than getting caught was nobody caring enough to catch me. On one occasion, my boy-friend and I, too young to drive but old enough and dumb enough to look for a dark place to hide, met up at the Royal for a matinee showing I knew would be sparsely populated. We scooted all the way to one side about ten rows down, virtually alone in the audi-torium. I didn't feel nearly as free as I'd hoped, however. The more we kissed, the more I worried that Dad would walk in and catch us, and I'd get in the worst trouble for acting naughty and being a bad girl. He'd been out when we'd come in.

Butterflies were starting to gather in my stomach, so I turned my head to make sure the coast was clear. And there he was. About six rows back, just watching us.

CHAPTER SIX

"GOOD MORNING TO THE BIGGEST CITY IN THE SOUTH!" Tony and I shot straight up in the back seat of the car to the abrupt awakening of KILT 610 radio. Dad needed the volume to shake the fatigue from his bones and the grogginess out of his head while he navigated four lanes of bumper-to-bumper traffic, the likes of which we'd never spied in our lives. He'd driven Mom, Tony, and me throughout the night hours down the endless monotony of I-10 West, all the way from Arkadelphia. The storms had not ended for us Greens, but the tornado that had spun our family madly for almost four years finally spit us out and landed us in the sprawling metroplex of Houston, Texas. It was just as well. The house on Twelfth was haunted now. Bad memories that hid behind the drapes during the day came out at night to hiss and dance and play. Dad was moving up in the world, not so much in salary as in status. He would oversee all the AMC multiscreen theaters in Houston, and there were no few.

The move was almost inexplicable. We were Arkansans and would be to our deaths. Our dearly departed were buried in Arkansas's loamy soil. Nearly all our living relatives were still there. Our heritage was there. The roots of the family trees of the Rountrees and the Greens plumbed the deepest depths of the rural hills of Arkansas from the time our ancestors migrated from America's eastern seaboard. For better and for worse, for both the richer and the poorer, it was home to our people. And one thing was startlingly clear. We were no longer home.

Tony and I stared speechless out the windows of the back seat, our bloodshot eyes big and round and the acid in our stomachs spitting flames. The sights and sounds were so foreign to us that we wouldn't have been much more startled had we awakened on Neptune. An 18-wheeler blared at Dad from behind, signaling for him to speed up or get out of the way. He got out of the way, rattled and, I'd imagine, wondering what on earth he was doing in that hot, congested city. It was late August, and the windows of businesses on both sides of the freeway were boarded up from a hurricane threat only a few days old. We'd come to die. That much was apparent to us.

We were still in yesterday's clothes, crumpled and sticky, and we were in considerable need of toothbrushes. Our parents had agreed, rather atypically, to drive through the night to allow Tony and me to attend going-away parties thrown by our friends. We'd sobbed into our pillows the first two hours of the drive until the cases were drenched, our bodies limp.

Nanny was back at the Ligon house overseeing the packing. Gay was in her freshman year at Henderson State in Arkadelphia.

We'd come at this precise time so Tony and I could start the school year in Houston. I was entering my sophomore year of high school and Tony, the eighth grade, and Mom had until midmorning to get us registered. We'd grab a quick lunch, then she and Dad would drop us off with church friends who'd moved to Houston several years earlier. Our parents would head back to Arkadelphia posthaste to finalize the sale of our house and facilitate the move. Tony and I would start school the very next day and stay with the Turners for several weeks.

That year Spring Woods High School in Houston, Texas, boasted some 4,700 students, spilling from the main building into a series of one-room structures they called T-shacks, T being short for *temporary*. The district would split the school the next year and, still, the head count would be three times the size of Arkadelphia High. When the bell rang at the end of each class, Spring Woods erupted like a cowboy boot had stomped an ant hill. It took weeks for me to get the hang of the hall traffic, continually going against the flow and getting hit so many times by massive sets of shoulders that I spun like a red plastic arrow on a game board. I learned fast that they grew dudes big in Texas. These guys were the size of the full-grown football players at Henderson and Ouachita. They ate stuff like chicken-fried steak and double-meat cheeseburgers for lunch and put chili on their fries. It was unseemly.

Tony's induction to Texas public schools was about the same. We'd have sobbed, whined, and woed-is-me fiercely if we hadn't been at the Turners', but we were guests under their roof and good manners severely limited our liberties.

Out of close to 4,700 kids, only a handful of them were Black. The sight was instantly conspicuous and surreal. By the time we left Arkadelphia, our public schools had been thoroughly integrated. Whatever admittedly small progress we had made in our friendships and classroom relationships back in Arkadelphia—nearness having become our new normal—we'd unfortunately no longer need to navigate in those early years in Houston. They'd claim they didn't have race problems in our school district, like avoidance wasn't a top-of-the-line name brand.

I'd not hear the term "white flight" for a couple of decades, but the week I entered my new school, I certainly beheld it. I didn't know what it was called, but as deep as my ignorance and my Arkansas-born-and-bred prejudices were, I knew something about it seemed sketchy. We had a bright-white welcome to suburban life in one of the most diverse cities in America. How does that make any sense to a newcomer? Just a few exits further west on I-10, you'll find yourself officially outside of Houston. The whole idea of progress in those days was to keep moving to the edges of the city.

● ● ●

Mom and Dad returned to Houston several weeks after dropping us off at the Turners' and closed on a home half the size of the Ligon house. They let Tony and me go back to Arkadelphia with them for the weekend to get Nanny and to load the rest of our belongings into a moving van.

That last afternoon, my best friend, Dodie, and our friend Mike swung by to pick me up so we could grab a bite at the Pig Pit Bar-B-Q before I left town. I ran across the front yard to remind my parents that we had discussed this and I'd be back in an hour and a half. They both began to protest. "The movers are too close to being ready to go and we need to drive right behind the van. You need to stay here so we're not waiting on you."

Whatever on God's green earth a conniption fit is, according to Mom and Dad, I threw one right then and there in the front yard. They'd dragged Tony and me from the only town we'd ever known and torn us away from all our friends, and we'd spent weeks in gargantuan new schools without a single family member, save each other. I was in no mood to be told no. Al and Aletha Green had picked a fine time to suddenly agree.

"No," they said in unison. "You're not going."

"But you promised!"

"We didn't know how close we'd be to leaving. The answer's no."

Mad as a hornet and heartbroken, I hugged my bosom friend, Dodie—the Diana to my Anne—goodbye. I'd miss her more than anyone. We'd shared a locker and our clothes and a trunkful of secrets. We'd painted our toenails the same colors and swore to one another we'd never let them go naked. I'd spent the night over at her house innumerable times and protected her from spending the night at mine. We neither one were angels, so we felt like lesser demons in our religious little town when we were together.

About a half hour later, as the last few boxes went into the moving van, we heard several sirens screaming bloody murder. We almost never heard more than one siren at a time in our town. All of us stopped what we were doing, turned an ear in the direction of the wailing ambulances, and listened with our eyebrows drawn.

"We need to wait!" I yelled. "It's gonna be somebody we know!"

My parents were exhausted, and with all the furniture in the van, there was no place to sit in the house. Nanny was eighty-six by now, and had she sat down on the front steps, she'd still be sitting there today as a pile of ashes. Dad swung open the car door to the back seat and shot me a serious look. "Get in, Beth. We've got to get on our way." I was on his last nerve and he, on mine.

Cell phones were unheard of. We had a brand-new telephone

number at the brand-new house we'd only owned for about a week, but none of our friends knew what it was. We hardly knew what it was. I went to school the next day and rode the bus home, still feeling immensely pouty at my unreasonable parents for not letting me go to the Pig Pit with my friends. When I walked through the front door, Mom and Nanny were sitting near one another on the couch. They both had tissues in their hands and the kind of pained looks on their faces that send every butterfly within ten square miles into an observer's stomach.

"Bethie, sit down with us a minute."

"No." I had no idea what they were about to say, but I was 100 percent positive I didn't want to hear it.

"Honey," Mom said, patting the space on the couch beside her, "come here."

I kept squeezing my eyes tight over and over like I could some-how make the surface of my brain so rigid and unyielding, the words wouldn't get in.

Dodie and Mike were dead. Just like that. He'd veered into the opposite lane, reaching for a pack of gum on the dashboard, just a mile or so from reaching the parking lot of the Pig Pit Bar-B-Q. Business as usual there. Customers stepping up to the counter. Cashier scribbling orders. "The two-meat special? Sliced beef, pork ribs, extra sauce. Side of baked beans and coleslaw. Got it. Pickles and sliced sweet onion are there by the silverware in the plastic containers. Fried blueberry pies will be out of the grease and on the counter in ten minutes, bubbling hot. Or you can have banana pudding if you've done lost your mind."

It was a head-on collision. Mike died instantly. Dodie's heart lived on for a few short hours. Of course it did. She was mostly heart. Her head injury, however, was catastrophic. From where I sat on the couch beside my mother, trying to process these two broken bodies of tender age, it seemed the whole world had lost its mind.

I still visit Dodie's grave when I'm in Arkadelphia and take daisies if I can find them. I round the small hill until I spy a certain memorial stone. It's the one with a built-in cameo picture of a fetching fifteen-year-old girl I knew as well as I knew myself, with a perfectly mischievous smile on her face. She gave her doting parents fits, and they didn't know the half of it. I pull off my shoes when I go to her grave and stand barefooted on the cold granite edge, the grass prickling my heels. "I'm still keeping my promise," I say. "Never a naked toe."

The death of a friend in childhood is so utterly unnatural that it leaves a fissure hard to mend. There was no going back now. The move was permanent. This strange, sprawling city, where the closest thing to an Arkansas hill was a concrete overpass, was our new home.

● ● ●

Mom and Dad were still at excruciating odds, but Mom's state of mind had undeniably improved with proof of Dad's infidelity.

Gay had stumbled on the evidence shortly before we moved from Arkadelphia. She was always half a detective. She was at the Royal that fateful afternoon and in need of a pen to jot down a note. She sat down at Dad's desk, and when she pulled out the long, shallow center drawer where Dad kept his colored pens, sharpened pencils, staple remover, and paper clips, her fingertips swept across a foreign object Scotch-taped to the underside of the drawer. She slid out of the chair and crouched under the desk to investigate. The way she saw it, anything taped somewhere top secret needed untaping.

It was a postmarked letter from Dad's girlfriend, four front-and-back handwritten pages on cutesy stationery. This was no one-night fling here. The words smelled to high heaven with the heavy perfume of familiarity, dripping with recent memories and imminent plans. Gay brought it straight home to me because that was how we did things. Pulled me by the arm into the bathroom so we could lock ourselves in. Slapped that envelope onto my palm. The folded sleeve was at least five months pregnant with pages, so I checked to see if the woman had used two stamps. That she had not cared a whit about robbing the post office of six cents told me all I needed to know. I combed through the innards, flipping the pages front to back.

"Holy moly," I said over and over.

"Oh, that's not all. Are you ready for this?" Gay asked.

"Yes!" And I was. God, help me, I was.

She held out two pictures, straight-armed like they were nailed to the blunt end of a two-by-four. Both were close-ups of the mistress and her pet, a white toy poodle. Her hair was short and frosted. By that I mean the mistress's, not the poodle's, though they did bear a remarkable resemblance. We'd struck gold, Gay and I.

"What do you think she thought Dad was going to do with those photos? Tack them to his bulletin board?"

"Don't ask me," I said, but she knew good and well I wanted her to.

Gay then gave me a stern and knowing look. It was the kind of look she got when she'd already made up her mind and a herd of buffaloes couldn't stop her. "We're calling her." She grabbed me by the wrist, unlocked the bathroom door, threw it open and swung me into the hall like a square-dance partner. "You get on this phone," she commanded, pointing to the black rotary on a shelf in the hall, "and I'll get on the one in the breakfast room."

"Wait, wait!" I pleaded. "Let's go over this first! What if Mom catches us?"

"She's *asleep*." Gay cocked her head and looked at me like *How dumb could you be?*

"But what about Nanny?"

"Nanny's gotten deaf as a stump. She won't know who we're talking to."

Oh, yes, she would. Nanny was a shameless snoop, and I was sure she only claimed to be hard of hearing so we'd drop our guard. But the fact was, she wouldn't have stopped us from making that call. Had there been a third phone, she'd have been on it. Still, I needed another minute to wrap my mind around what we two teenagers were about to do.

"How are we going to get ahold of her?" I asked.

Gay held up the envelope and pecked her index finger at the upper left-hand corner, where the return address was written in curly cursive with a bright-blue Bic: first name, last name, street address, and city. "We're calling directory assistance for this name and address in Memphis, Tennessee!"

And we did. It was like taking candy from a baby. We scratched down the tawdry digits as fast as the operator could spit them out.

"Helllllllo." Took that Tennessee woman ten seconds and four full syllables just to answer the phone, me writhing in the hall.

Gay started in right away. "You better never see our dad again as long as you live."

"Who is this?" she asked, like she didn't know.

"*Who is this?* You want to know who this is? I'll tell you who this is! This is me, Gay Green, and this is my sister, Beth Green."

A few seconds passed before I realized this was my cue. Then I piped up. "Yeah!"

Gay would make a statement punctuated with phone-splattering plosives, then say, "Right, Beth?"

"Yeah!"

"And I'll tell you another thing." And she would.

When she paused, I'd say, "Yeah!"

Gay told the woman what she thought of her disgusting poodle.

"Yeah!" And I meant every word of it.

That Jezebel had the gall to try to sweet-talk us and tell us what good friends we were going to be someday. She may as well have unleashed a rabid Rottweiler in her den. I couldn't see my big sister, but I knew by now she must be foaming at the mouth. If Gay said *over our dead bodies* once to the woman, she said it a dozen times.

I don't recollect exactly how the call ended, but no one need wonder if Gay got the last word. She came whirling around the corner of the breakfast room and into the hall like Superwoman, cape flapping. I never saw anyone fiercer. "Can you believe the nerve of that woman?"

"No," I said, the hair on my arms standing straight up.

"She thinks she's gonna marry Dad."

I could not fathom for the life of me why either of those two women—the one with the toy poodle or the one sound asleep in the bed in broad daylight—wanted to be married to Dad. It was sheer mystery.

Gay and I stood in the hall and shook our heads for a moment. I feel sure Gay cussed, but I was still shy at cussing. I'd been a bit awkward on the call and something needed to be said, so I just went ahead and said it. "I felt like my yeahs got meaner and meaner."

"They did," Gay agreed, "they surely did. Meaner'n a snake."

She knew better. She knew I was the biggest chicken in the

Green farmyard. But that's how she was with me. Every kid needs somebody like that. I'd remind Gay over and over years later when we were well into the throes of adulthood, "You were the brave one. Not me. It was always you. You can do anything you put your mind to."

"We're telling Mom." That's what Gay said next in the hall, gaining steam from making a long-distance call all the way to Memphis, Tennessee, not caring a hoot in Hogscald Holler that Dad was going to find out about it and, better yet, pay the phone bill for it. Sure enough, she told Mom, and I said yeah.

• • •

Strange, how the most unwanted things can become gifts. Mom didn't feel nearly as much like dying once we knew who'd been lying. She didn't even feel as much like sleeping. In fact, she was feeling better altogether, at least for a while. Vindication can be a powerful elixir. Things were looking up now that she had something definitive on Dad. Now that she knew she wasn't crazy. Now that her children believed her. Nothing feels better than knowing, even for just a clear minute, you aren't crazy after all. I don't doubt she got a permanent and some fresh hair color right after this.

I wish I'd heard it with my own ears. It would've been scrumptious tonic. I don't know for a fact Mom said it, but I can't picture that she didn't, given the opportunity. Here's how I imagine it:

"The kids know. They know I didn't make it up. They know what kind of man you've been." Lord-a-mercy, we knew what kind of man Dad had been better than Mom did. Still, I'd like to have heard her say "they believe me" and seen his face when he heard it.

Now, I don't know what Dad would've said to Mom's version of *I told you so*, but it wouldn't have mattered. Sometimes you just get to know you were right even if the other person denies it.

Mom was in a strange new place in no few ways. Dad couldn't just strut around like a peacock without knowing we spied with our little eyes one very serious player. Oh, he'd still strut around often enough, but without the applause of a certain conspicuous section of his audience.

Gay hadn't moved with us to Houston. Not yet, anyway. But the woman who'd birthed us both—Esther Aletha Rountree Green—made the move, not exactly wearing a cape, but no longer searching barefooted for the nearest river.

Mom didn't leave Dad then, nor would she leave him later when she learned of more grievous transgressions. She sentenced him instead to infernally long bouts of solitary confinement under the same roof with her. Don't imagine this to be a light sentence. I still daydream from time to time about what our lives might have been like if Mom had left Dad. I thought about it incessantly the week we seven celebrated their fiftieth wedding anniversary.

My mother didn't see leaving as a viable option. She never once brought it up, to my knowledge. In her reality—whether actual or perceived—where was she to go and what, exactly, was she to do to support herself? She had a high school education, checks bouncing like rubber balls, an elderly mother, one kid in college and two more kids to go, and all without a whit of confidence in herself. She also had a recent history of mental instability, though such considerations didn't likely factor into the equation. No, Mom did what many women of her era did. She stayed, despite a dozen valid reasons to go. She considered dying, but never leaving. She was never under threat of Dad taking her to court for custody. Lawyers were for people with money, and Dad was by no means looking to spend money—we didn't have it, anyway—or raise kids. Among other dark things, he appeared, at least to me, to simply want Mom to slip out of the picture so he could enlist someone new to raise us.

He wouldn't get the chance, you can bet your toy poodle on that.

CHAPTER SEVEN

WE DON'T ALWAYS WANT A NEW START, no matter how badly we need one. A new beginning can come for us like an intruder breaking into our house—into our very lives as we know them—and drag us kicking and screaming into a place inhospitable to our previous selves. A place where our skin doesn't even seem to fit the same way around our bones. A place where we stare both out the window and in the mirror, looking for comforts of familiarity. Whether we are going to change isn't an option here. The only option is what kind of change we're going to make.

Houston was that intruder to me, that killer captor come to take me somewhere I didn't think I wanted to go. I could not see it then, but I'd catch enough glimpses of God's providence in my peripheral vision to suspect, before long, that he'd moved us himself so that we could find a sustainable life. Our Arkansas town wasn't the problem. We loved Arkadelphia. I still love it and long for its hills and pines. The injuries our family incurred there were the problem. And when enough hardship happens within a small circumference, the roads to all the familiar places are little more than crisscrossing scars. By the time every direction you could take at a four-way stop—right, left, straight ahead, or reverse—carries the stomach-turning scent of carnage, moving can mean surviving.

I was about to get to start over. Mind you, for those who have lived past third grade, there's no real starting over from scratch. There's just starting over *scratched*—and if the hurts clawed deep enough, *scarred*. But for those who resist insisting on idyllic circumstances and faultless people, new beginnings can be had.

Our family had been reduced to so few in a community of so many, even once we settled into a house and a neighborhood, that we no longer had any notion of who we were. The oddity for me, at fifteen years of age, was the fact that resigning myself to that nothingness, to that lostness and invisibleness, was an almost instant relief. For one thing, I could wash my face and leave it bare, and who was going to care? You don't have to hide anything when you're invisible. I began my sophomore year wearing no makeup at all. Having no friends at all. No small-town popularity, which meant, gloriously, that there was also no small-town, overnight *un*popularity.

I was accustomed to a miserable social order of perpetual musical chairs. All the "in" people couldn't be in at the same time, lest small town life be too boring, so every day the music played and when it stopped, somebody wasn't going to have a chair. You wouldn't even know what you'd done. You'd just go to school the next day and none of your crowd would be talking to you.

Those early days at Spring Woods High, no one was talking to me anyway. I was no longer cool or uncool. No longer in or out. The sheer mass of bodies maneuvering the corridors and classrooms meant no one even knew who was new. I didn't, however, stay anonymous in my classrooms for long. A month was about as long as I could keep from participating in class in the subjects I loved.

One late September day, our English teacher asked the class a question like she did every day. Only this particular day, my hand shot up in the air like it had a mind of its own. Since I'd been mute up to now, she called on me without hesitation. The second I opened my mouth and uttered the first sentence, laughter roared over my gravy-thick Arkansas accent. Why this did not shut me up is a mystery. Alas, I endured. My classmates finally got to the point that, when I raised my hand, they'd chant to the teacher, "Call on her! Call on her!" The ridicule never stopped, but somewhere along the way it lost its sharp teeth, and they mostly just gummed me half to death.

I did okay in my classes because knowing people wasn't imperative. But as it is for every outsider, lunch was brutal. The eight most spectacular words falling on the ear of a lonely kid clutching a tray: "You can sit with us if you want."

She scooted down the bench of the picnic-style table in the commons, where students ate lunch. The girls to her left followed her lead, crowding in together.

"What's your name?"

"Beth Green."

And they told me theirs. I ate with them the next day and the next.

My friendships and associations underwent complete reconstruction with the move to Houston, and largely for the better. I'd never again be pigeonholed into one group of people. The road to reconstruction wasn't without a few bumps, however. After living in Houston several months, a couple of girls asked me to spend an upcoming Friday night at one of their homes.

"I don't know what I should do," I told my mom.

"Do you like them?"

"Yes, ma'am. I don't know them very well, but they seem fun."

"Then, honey, go! It's new friends!"

Nanny chimed in. "Letha, you ain't gone further than the grocer's whole time we been here. Reckon how you gonna find some stranger's house?"

"They'll gimme directions, Nanny. We'll find it," I said. "We're gonna have to find our way around sooner or later."

"I guess I can call the police when your momma don't come home 'fore mornin'."

I guessed we got to be the kind of people who call the police now since nobody knew us here in the big city.

Come Friday evening, I read the directions while Mom navigated the intersections with a fair amount of anxiety and a thick fog of burning tobacco. It was nearly November, but still hot as blue blazes. We pictured how the hills around Arkadelphia would be a patchwork of autumn colors by now and moaned for home.

My two new friends came bopping out the front door in their low-rise bell-bottoms as soon as we drove up, probably because Mom squealed the tires overcorrecting the way she'd hit the curb and nearly taken out their mailbox. People in Houston put their mailboxes too close to the street. The girls were freckle-faced and darling and mannerly enough that I knew Mom would be impressed with them. I met Kim's mom and small-talked for a moment, primarily answering questions.

"Yes, ma'am. Just a couple of months."

"Yes, ma'am, from Arkansas."

"No, ma'am, I don't have to call you ma'am if you don't want me to."

"Arkadelphia. It's a small college town outside Little Rock."

"Only five of us moved here but I'm from a family of eight. My grandmother lives with us."

"He manages movie theaters."

"Yes, ma'am, I do like movies."

"My favorite? *Love Story*? Well, yes, I did like it." I really didn't because I thought love ought to mean saying a million sorrys, but I suddenly felt odd about admitting I preferred *Count Dracula*, the 1970 release, for its honesty.

Soon we three fifteen-year-old girls were off to Kim's bedroom. I'd barely crossed the threshold when she shut the door behind us and locked it. I wasn't sure I'd ever seen an actual lock on a bedroom door. I thought how I could have used one of those. Kim made a beeline straight to her chest of drawers, dug around in the bottom, pulled out a plastic bag of what appeared to be catnip, raised her bedroom window, and lit up a joint.

I expected an armed raid any second and pictured how I was going to have to write letters to Nanny from prison. I did my best not to let on. I just acted like it was an everyday thing for your mother to be in the den ten feet down the hall watching *The Partridge Family* while you and your spend-the-night company are about to go to the pen. We stayed perfectly friendly at school after that, but I mostly spent nights at home until I could get a few things figured out.

Then there was my first date in Houston. A young man from one of my classes asked me out. He said we could hang out with a group of kids from Spring Woods and I'd have a chance to get to know a lot of people. Though I didn't have any romantic feelings for him, I also didn't have many friends or any plans. He didn't seem like an axe murderer and, as far as I could tell, was too shy to be handsy, so I went, and he was right. We did meet up with his friends—but at a nightclub. A real live nightclub. Why on earth they let a group of high school sophomores through the door remains perplexing. We might as well have been in Las Vegas, if you asked me.

I was so nervous, I never got up from the table. The music blared, so I also didn't talk. I just nodded and sipped on something tall, red, and slushy my date called a hurricane. As I live and breathe, I couldn't taste a hint of alcohol in it. When it was time to go, I had no feet at all. Lord-a-mercy, I had no knees. I had to be carried to the car. All I remember on the drive home was hollering for him to stop. I flung the door open and threw up rivers of red right there in public on the pavement of the 7-Eleven. Possessing a strong aversion to public vomiting, I have this one incident to thank for keeping me stone-cold sober through the rest of high school and all through college, and for teetotaling my way into adulthood.

● ● ●

With the move and the sudden luxury of big-city anonymity, my parents dropped out of church. The about-face was a whiplash, especially for Nanny. She pined for it something fierce, but she was simultaneously getting less and less mobile. Basics like getting in and out of the car had grown difficult.

I made a decision that seemed small at the time. I decided to go to church by myself. I had no idea where to go. The Turners attended First Baptist Church of Spring Branch, and they had taken Tony and me with them while we stayed at their house. That seemed the natural choice, but it wasn't nearly as close to our home as theirs. Still, I mustered the courage to call Mrs. Turner and ask her if they could give me a ride. They were dear enough to say yes without hesitation.

Mom found it understandably awkward and soon offered to start taking me and picking me up herself. I kept thinking, *Any week now she's going to say, "Well, I will just go in with you,"* but she never did. I think she knew Dad would have jumped back in immediately and gotten involved up to his neck, and she'd lost her tolerance for hypocrisy.

Mom and Dad's relationship was still in shambles in the fresh wake of the exposed affair. Though Dad swore it was over, Mom had no way of knowing for certain. The phone would occasionally ring and, when we'd answer, the caller would sit in silence for several moments, then hang up. A saint couldn't have kept from wondering if it was her, and we were no saints. We were scarred enough that for months to come, nothing seemed black-and-white. Nothing was certain. Everything was colored with suspicion.

My parents would go back to church eventually but not until after I'd finished high school. In time I got my learner's permit and was in line at the Texas Department of Public Safety by 9 a.m. the morning of my sixteenth birthday to get my driver's license.

From then on, Mom let me borrow their black-and-yellow Dodge Dart to go to church and sometimes to school. It was like driving around a yellowjacket, but I didn't care. It was dependable enough if you kept a gallon milk jug full of water on the floorboard of the back seat on account of the radiator's deep commitment to overheating. I knew just how to pop the hood and cool it off if necessary, and if we drove it over thirty minutes in the heat with the AC on, it was rarely unnecessary.

I got involved in the church youth group and choir and the like, going to camp and on missions trips. Every now and then we'd have a special service where the students either spoke or sang, and my parents would come. Other than that, I was on my own, church-wise, those three high school years in Houston. It was a time of deciding rather than having everything decided for me. I now lived in a city where *not* going to church was far more common than going. You could say you believed in God without doing a single thing to show it.

I would decide over those three years who I wanted to be. Mind you, I would not become that person for years, if ever at all. There would be no arriving, just pursuing. It wasn't so much three steps forward and two steps back as it was ten thousand steps in circles and cycles. I would wonder if it was still considered hypocrisy if the person I pretended to be was the person I deeply wanted to be. Of course I knew the answer. The guilt of duplicity would consume me at times. I'd repent, sorrowfully and earnestly, over what seemed inevitable patterns of stupid choices. I'd promise God to do better and I'd keep it up for a while. Then, sooner or later, I'd repeat the same old cycle of self-sabotage. In every sense of the saying, I could not keep my act together.

Somehow in the mess of it, Jesus stayed. He kept his commitment to me when I was at a loss to consistently keep what seemed a single commitment to him.

A teenager doesn't know she's still a child. A teenager feels like an adult, I suppose primarily because her outside, her flesh and her face, her body, her size, her width and height, look like—and can function like, get pregnant like, can party like, get arrested like, and die just like—an adult. She thinks she's making decisions as a grown-up with a fully developed brain and, in a case like mine, a fully developed faith. She's wrong about both of those beliefs. But chances are, she will not realize what a child she was until, as a full-grown adult, she knows and loves a teenager.

I kept going to church, bouts of hypocrisy and all. Kept going to those student activities. Kept singing in the choir. Kept taking my offering envelope with a couple of folded-up dollar bills in it. Kept volunteering to read the passage aloud in my high school Sunday school class.

What I could not see for the life of me was that one-half of the duplicitous person mocking me in the bathroom mirror and telling me what a fake I was had something on the other half. Something that continued to drive a black-and-yellow Dodge Dart with a faulty radiator back and forth to a community of faith. It was called hope.

CHAPTER EIGHT

Nanny died of a stroke on the furthest thing from a feather mattress in a hospital room in Houston, just as the azaleas were blooming our first early spring. We might have found a dogwood to drive her by, had she given us more notice. The only familiar sight before her soul fled her world-worn body was the face of her daughter. No face would have been lovelier to her and no fragrance homier than Mom's Estée Lauder Youth-Dew with a touch of smoke, but what I wouldn't give to rewrite Nanny's ending with us all in the room walking her home, singing. Perhaps what she needed more than people was peace. We Greens were a lot of things, but no one ever accused us of being a peaceful lot. I'd not only rewrite her story with a crowded room, I'd rewind the clock seven months and forfeit all that time just for her to have the comfort of dying in the town she—and we—still called home.

Minnie Ola Steed first blinked her eyes to the light of day on March 1, 1886, nestled in the arms of her mother, Aletha Jane, for whom she'd later name her daughter. No other scenario makes sense but that Nanny came fresh from the womb considerably contrary. Contrariness was her lifelong love language and, once you accepted it as such, oddly comforting. Her birthplace is on record simply as Pike County, since she was born and raised miles from a town with a post office. The tiny farming community did, however, have a name. The early settlers called it Pisgah after a location mentioned in the closing scene of Deuteronomy. I can't speak for the ancient Israelites, but the only acceptable pronunciation for Arkansans from our place that was called by the same name is *PIZZ-gy*. Here's how the Bible story goes:

> Then Moses went up from the plains of Moab to Mount
> Nebo, to the top of Pisgah, which faces Jericho, and the
> LORD showed him all the land. . . . The LORD then said
> to him, "This is the land I promised Abraham, Isaac, and
> Jacob, 'I will give it to your descendants.' I have let you
> see it with your own eyes, but you will not cross into it."
>
> So Moses the servant of the LORD died there in the
> land of Moab, according to the LORD's word. He buried
> him in the valley in the land of Moab facing Beth-peor,
> and no one to this day knows where his grave is.
>
> DEUTERONOMY 34:1, 4-6

Now, God is God and can do what he pleases, and God knows he's always right and righteous and wise. But, having sinned considerably in my lifetime, I can only feel sorry for Moses for not getting to go to the Promised Land on account of how he'd smacked the rock twice, frustrated to no end with the confounding people demanding water, after God had told him to speak to it (Numbers 20:7-12). Moses isn't the only one who preferred smacking to speaking. But just about the time I'd think Moses had lost God's favor and breathed his last with God perturbed at him, there God is, burying him. God, who'd dug a garden in Eden with his own hands in Genesis 2:8, where he placed the man he'd formed from the dust of the ground, took those same hands and dug a hole overlooking the Promised Land and picked up the 120-year-old lifeless body of his servant, laid him in it, and covered it there with his hand. If that's not love, I don't know it.

The ink dries permanently on the thick scroll of Deuteronomy with this epitaph. "No prophet has arisen again in Israel like Moses, whom the LORD knew face to face" (Deuteronomy 34:10).

I have to think bodies matter to the Maker of heaven and earth only second to souls. He formed these human bodies of ours meticulously if curiously. Considering all we have going on inside of us at once, the wonder is not that we get sick but that we spend ten consecutive minutes *well*. To my people, not only did a body matter, where a body was laid to rest mattered. They took the ancient practice of being buried with the fathers seriously (Genesis 49:29). No way was Nanny going to be at rest within earshot of honking 18-wheelers on Houston freeways, nor would she have cared to be in a hundred-degree oven every summer of her dead life. Mom didn't care what the price tag was, and Dad didn't likely either. Without question or discussion, Nanny's body was going back to Arkansas where it belonged.

Something about standing over the lifeless body of the person who braved the valley of the shadow of death—panting, wincing, sweating, yelping, pushing, and bleeding—to give you life is particularly poignant. I believe this to be true even where relationships have ruptured, weakened, or altogether severed.

Dad came home first to tell us Nanny was gone. He was not at all cold. He knew a major figure in all our lives, his included, had just vanished from our landscape. No one in our expansive family was less anonymous than Nanny. A few hours later Mom walked through the door, tears dripping from her jaw, moving slowly through the entryway and den toward the kitchen like the least bump against a piece of furniture would tear open her flesh and bleed her out. My mother was fifty when Nanny died and had lived with her precisely fifty years. Everywhere my family moved, Nanny moved with us. Though Mom had to have seen it coming and knew what a struggle daily tasks had become for Nanny, she was devastated by her death.

I cannot recall hugging my mother at that moment. If my memory is accurate, I stood back, staring, frozen in place like all ten of my fingertips were lead weights. I wish I could do it over again and hold her in my arms this time and comfort her and tell her how sorry I am and affirm what a loss she'd suffered even if I felt awkward. I wish I'd made it to the kettle before she did and told her to rest on the couch and let me serve her. I should have lit her cigarette for her. I don't know why I didn't. She had not raised uncompassionate children. All five of us were sentimental. I hugged her a thousand other times in the years that followed, swift with words of consolation, but that moment in a house in Houston that still felt like an ill-fitting shoe, all I recall is paralysis. Perhaps I was terrified that a wave of grief this size and this soon after she'd emerged from the ocean floor would drown her. I went in my bedroom alone with the loss, closed the door, and sobbed.

• • •

I have no recollection of our drive back to Arkansas for the funeral and burial, but Wayne, in Houston at the time, made the trip with us and remembers it distinctly. He tells me the only sound in the car was Mom sniffling. It goes without saying that Dad also snorted on account of his apparently untreatable postnasal drip, but beyond that, Mom got what she wanted. Quiet. No radio. No incessant chatter from her children. Just silence.

After four or five hours, the quiet had grown intolerable and Dad finally asked, "Couldn't we please just turn on a little radio?" She guessed so. Wayne reports that a few minutes later, the Four Tops came on singing their latest hit gleefully like they didn't care an iota what anybody listening was going through. If you wanted a dirge, you weren't going to get it from the Four Tops. Wayne says Mom lasted through it as long as she could then switched it off with significant fervor. With one sob per syllable, she blurted out, "My mother has died, and I don't wanna hear 'Ain't No Woman Like the One I Got'!"

This kind of thing—the way we Greens could dramatize—is what my family did best. Of all the things handed down through our family line, this may well be what I appreciate most. Before you go feeling sorry for my mother for having such disrespectful children that they had to bite their lips to keep from bursting out laughing, I'd slap a clean and crispy ten-dollar bill on the table to bet she had to stare out the front passenger window and pinch her own lips to keep from doing the same. It's how we did things, and not a one of us has ever been sorry enough to change.

There's no real explaining what got into those early settlers' minds when they named my grandmother's homeland after the mountaintop where God gave Moses a panoramic view of the

Promised Land. Arkansas has a generous share of mountain ranges, but not in those parts. Those parts are gentle hills with trees enough to make you strain to see the sunset; nevertheless, Pisgah it was and Pisgah it stayed, and I suppose everybody has a right to consider any plot of land hospitable enough to build their lives upon as being just a stone's throw from God's favorite. Pisgah was our favorite, anyway, and if it was good enough for Moses, it was good enough for Nanny.

We tucked Nanny's body into a bed of earth two days later, exactly where she wanted to be buried. We returned her to the same Arkansas clay where her life had begun and to the cemetery adjoined to her old church. That's how they did it back in that day, and who's to say it wasn't a good way? There was no distance at all between where they came to faith and where they came to rest, where they gathered for worship and where they gathered to wail, where they ate on the grounds after church and where they ate the food of tears. Sanctuary and cemetery, where they held flowers and married and where they laid flowers and buried.

She was finally at her husband's side. Her fiddle-playing, foot-tapping man raised on the same hills, graduated from Mountain Home College and the University of Arkansas law school, a practicing lawyer who served as a small-town mayor, then in the Arkansas House of Representatives for three terms, the last of which he held until his death. When his occupation necessitated a move closer to the state capitol, he'd sent her and my mom, a tiny thing at the time, to Arkadelphia, while he walked their cow thirty-three winding, rising, dipping, daunting country miles. He died when my mom was fourteen. Nanny never remarried, pining for long, tall Micajah Rountree the rest of her life.

They were together now, their bodies in sweet repose under a thick blanket of earth right beside the graves of Esna Irene, their firstborn, who breathed her last at six weeks old; Prentis, their second born, who left their arms empty at two years of age; and Anthony Dalton, their sixth born, also two, and whose death, Nanny claimed, nearly put his grief-racked parents and three big brothers in the grave with him. I don't know how a human heart keeps beating after such crushing. My mother was their seventh and last. When Minnie Ola Rountree and her brown-eyed daisy, Esther Aletha, climbed aboard that carriage for the big city of Arkadelphia, she must have had the fortitude of ten men for the reins tied to those three graves not to pull her clean off the seat.

● ● ●

Words have a life of their own. When we no longer have the warm body of someone we loved, if they lived long enough to speak and spoke often enough in our hearing, they have a way of living on through language. Their words are right there, floating in the air, ready to wet the tongue as a moment arises when you know good and well what they'd say. My siblings and I speak fluent Nanny-ese. We can go whole conversations without speaking a single original word. This is the gift of having lived within the same walls. She never had no comment.

We had to stand ankle-deep in the stream of her legacy and pan the gold from the gravel for what was worth saving. Worth passing on. Some words and ways we each wanted to keep, but some needed condemning to the pit of hell. Racism ran through my grandmother's red blood like orange iron.

To her, desegregation was practically a death sentence. Her aversion was fed by raw, unfiltered fear. According to Nanny, Black people were going to multiply and slaughter white people and take over. Holding on to an ugly and erroneous historical narrative, in her mind we were the victims, not they. To her, we had not taken what was theirs; they were coming to take what was ours.

I knew, even as a young child back at the Royal Theater, that my Black classmates having to climb those narrow stairs to a separate space was immoral. The Black students at our high school in Arkadelphia had names. Parents. Churches. Many among them were personal friends. And yet every morning my sister and I walked across Twelfth Street to the school, Nanny watched us from the picture window, certain one of the boys with deep-brown skin sitting on the steps up to the school door was going to grab us. The unavoidable irony was in the notion that our home—with all of its heinous secrets—was safe, but crossing the street would get us molested.

"Nanny, good grief, nobody's gonna get us!" we'd say repeatedly, only for it to fall on deaf ears. Jesus spoke of people who had ears but would not hear and eyes but would not see. To people in my grandmother's likeness, those boys were not image bearers. They were as feared as werewolves out for prey in broad daylight.

As ignorant as we five children were about matters of injustice and inequality, and as deeply steeped as we were in 1960s and 1970s white culture, we knew when she talked the way she did that she was wrong. *Hateful.* We were skewed enough to believe, to our shame, that a certain amount of racism was acceptable, "normal." But we were not blind enough—our young consciences not yet seared enough—to think Nanny hadn't crossed that line by a country mile. Unmistakably, our religious grandmother, who read the Bible on her bedside table every night, who loved Sunday school and church and wept through every hymn, had a deep and appalling gash of hypocrisy in the armor of her piety. You know some things in your gut. You don't have to take an ethics course. You don't have to know God well to know that, if he is righteous at all, some things are wrong. If he is good at all, some things are evil. If God is love, then nothing is more blasphemous than hate.

• • •

There was nothing to love and everything repelling in the racist Nanny, a good bit to resist in the critical Nanny, but to a handful of kids clamoring for stability, the comically rural and ever-available Nanny was worth a heap.

Something was comforting about how Nanny never shed her hick vernacular. The continuous squabbles between her nouns and verbs were things a soul could count on. The way she pronounced *can't* as if it rhymed with *ain't* was classic. It felt good and fitting and rounded out. Her figures of speech weren't lifted from books. Their origins were stories. They were sensory and earthy, connected, like a spade in garden soil, like a baby at a breast.

She quilted, cracked pecans, shelled peas, fished for perch. She was so bent on cooking the trichinosis out of a pound of meat that every roast we ate was burned to a crisp and every piece of patty sausage curled up into a tiny bowl. The latter proved beneficial in that it would hold a tablespoon of gravy without spilling a drop so we could pick it up and eat it in one bite.

Burying Nanny had some mild advantages, although the house had too big a hole in it for us to appreciate them. Sticking her in a coffin meant the end of her incessant compulsion to consolidate. Once the breakfast cereal boxes were only a third full, she combined them all into one box. Being pleasant in the morning with one's elderly grandmother was a challenging prospect after pouring a bowlful of Cap'n Crunch that turned out to be equal parts Grape-Nuts and Special K. Same for chips. The Fritos, Lay's, and Cheetos were all destined for the same bag. Same for plastic bottles of soda pop in the refrigerator. It was one thing to order a suicide back at the Royal; it was another thing to happen on it. We'd come in from school and head to the kitchen for an afternoon snack and, seconds later, nine times out of ten, one word could be heard reverberating through the house. "Naaaaaaaaanny!"

Hers was the gift of presence. She was simply always there. Always there on Saturday nights with pin curls in her wispy gray hair upon which she was going to put a hat come Sunday morning for church. Always there, spit-washing a smudge off our faces, even when we were in high school. Always there in front of the oven with mitts on both hands waiting to pull out something hot, her wide hips eclipsing the oven door and with her dress caught at times where the sun don't shine. Always there on the other phone eavesdropping on our conversations. Always there with an "Ain'tcha hungry?" and, when we said yes because we almost always were, spreading butter on a slice of light bread, folding it over and handing it to us like a feast. And it was.

"Want sugar on it?"

"No, ma'am." Then again, sometimes, "Yes, ma'am." It was mood dependent. Two different tastes entirely.

A month before she died, my parents had to leave town for Dad's job and I'd just had a stomach virus I couldn't shake. On day three when I still had no appetite and was ghost-pale, she sat on the couch with me, scraped the inside of a ripe apple with a small spoon and hand-fed me until I was well.

Nanny was there. That's all. And then she wasn't. No more story to it than that.

CHAPTER NINE

I FOLLOWED THE TURNERS TO CHURCH, then after graduating from high school, I followed their younger daughter, Sandy, to college in San Marcos. She was a senior at what was then called Southwest Texas State University (now called Texas State) when I was an incoming freshman. Situated quaintly in the hill country with a clear, green river coursing through its center, San Marcos was a natural pick for a couple of Arkansans. Going back to Arkansas for college wasn't an option for me because out-of-state tuition was outside our budget, and at that time, SWTSU was as low-dollar as a state university could get. It also accepted practically anybody, and practicality was precisely what I needed.

My grades, which plummeted my freshman year of high school in the hub of the Green tornado, stayed wobbly through my transitional sophomore year but found some muscle during my junior and senior years. By that time I'd adapted, made friends, gotten involved in extracurricular activities, and fallen for a pretty wonderful guy who single-handedly packed my last two years of high school with great memories. I never told him anything about my family's history. He had a real live healthy family with solid, traditional values. These were the Cleavers. They didn't cuss, smoke, drink, or even fight. His dad was a bank president who came home every Monday through Friday for a sit-down lunch prepared by a stay-at-home mom who, as far as I know, didn't even take a nap. His family went to church every Sunday and lived their quiet faith Monday through Saturday.

The way I saw it, these people had everything on earth—except the ability to deal with my ugly truth. So I did what most troubled teenage girls do who are trying to be somebody new. I shoved the door shut on the past. And no matter how the wood bulged, the bones rattled, or the knob turned from within, I pressed my back against that door, tried to talk over the noise, and dug in my heels with every ounce of determination I had. My high school boyfriend and I chose different universities and only lasted long-distance for a little less than a semester. We'd take another shot at it later, but the same shame still haunted me. We weren't a match. I figured if I married him, I'd spend my life pretending I'd been something I wasn't.

I jumped into college life like a cat on all fours, trying out for drill team before my clothes were unpacked and pledging a sorority shortly after. I majored in political science on a pre-law track in hopes of following in my grandfather Micajah's footsteps. Our university drill team performed at football games, so my parents would make the three-hour drive at least once a month to see our halftime show.

I started noticing almost immediately that the temperature between them wasn't quite as glacial. Lo and behold, they'd found a church ten minutes from our home. Dad started going first, and in what I can only attribute to an act of God, talked Mom and Tony into visiting with him. They fell equally in love with it, and just like that, the Greens were back to Sunday mornings, Sunday evenings, Wednesday night potluck suppers and prayer meetings. On weekends home, I forsook the church I'd attended by myself in high school and, in solidarity, began to attend Spring Woods Baptist with my parents and little brother. They were right. It was a warm and happy, servant-hearted congregation.

● ● ●

With our family's new start, I managed to create a new narrative so entirely self-convincing, it showed up with inexplicable sincerity in my prayers. Decades later, when my husband and I were packing up our city lives and moving to the country, I found my very first prayer journal at the bottom of a musty cardboard box Keith dropped from the attic. I flicked a dead spider off the small, bright-red three-ring binder and wiped a thick layer of dust off the vinyl surface with my fingertips. The words *Spiritual Daybook* emerged, typeset around the logo of a cross.

"Oh, wait a minute. I remember this."

I opened the cover to several pages of basic journaling instructions fronting a thick stack of miniature notebook paper. My name and a start date were written in my neatest penmanship in a fill-in-the-blank on the first page. I did the math and smiled. I was eighteen. Since I didn't write in it every day, it contained notes spanning several years of college.

I sat cross-legged on the floor, loosed the moorings of a

thousand pressing tasks, and sailed back in time to my late adolescent life, recorded through reams of prayers. Some of the entries were so earnest and naive, so oblivious to what was ahead, they sent tears tumbling down my face. I snatched a roll of toilet tissue from the upstairs bathroom and laced my lap with crumpled wads, wet with tears. I half wished to hold that young Beth in my arms like a mother and tell her I loved her because I never, ever told her back then. Never gave her any slack. I've had mixed feelings about her at every stage. Other entries were so unwittingly absurd and hilarious, I fell over on my side and laughed until my stomach cramped. Some of the recordings weren't far from the kinds of things I had prayed that morning, and I wasn't sure if that was good news or bad. A cross section of entries:

"Help me keep up my enthusiasm so I'll be a better Christian."

"Forgive me for being too bossy."

"Forgive me for talking about other people and for gossiping too much." (Oh, that I'd recorded the gossip.)

"Help me not to be a 'repeat offender.'" (The fact that *repeat offender* was in quotations indicates I'd heard it in a sermon, and whatever it was, I most assuredly did not want to be guilty of it.)

"Help me conquer these feelings I have."

"Forgive me for talking so much."

"Don't let me hurt anyone else."

"Help me to be a good Christian and not give in to temptation."

"Forgive me for losing my temper."

"Please help me have a better disposition."

"Forgive me for not being the Christian I should be 100% of the time." (Somebody needed to help the girl out.)

What I'd written didn't astound me nearly as much as what I hadn't. I'd bleached my family story of all blatant references to turmoil. I've faked a number of things in my life to get by, but

I've always had a ripe fear of God, far too much to lie to him to his face, yet there it was, in my eighteen-, nineteen-, and twenty-year-old handwriting: a whole new family narrative.

On my birthday: "Thank you for a stable and happy home. I pray that I'll be a better and happier person this next year."

"Praise God for having me born into such a wonderful family."

"Help me get out of this state of uneasiness and always being about to cry. Thank you for the help my family has been to me."

"Thank you for the fun our family has together." (And on occasion and in certain groupings, nothing could have been truer.)

"Thanks for my mom. She's always here and I love her so much." (And she *was* there again.)

I thanked God repeatedly in the journal pages for "my wonderful parents" and told him how blessed I was to be born into such a good family. A godly family.

I love my family of origin. I loved it then. I had every reason to be grateful to God for the miracle that appeared to be underway in my home, and God knows I believed in the power of the gospel to transform lives. The oddity was that my words betrayed no hint that things had ever been different. Not a whiff of the acrid darkness from which we were being delivered. No before and after. The omissions were mystifying.

Maybe it was my idea of how a clean slate should look for a Jesus follower, completely homogenizing *forgiving* and *forgetting*. Maybe it was a way of keeping no record of wrongs. Whatever it was, I'd not just shut the trauma in. I'd shut it out. Poof. Gone. Almost overnight.

Any references made to conflicts, both within and without, were completely detached from the old narrative. It wasn't so much that I'd forgotten the trauma as that I refused to remember. My past and present had made a deal and shaken on it. "I won't bother you if you won't bother me." Our family had been reborn. Never mind how much we still looked like our old selves.

The irony was in the bold sincerity of my dissimulation. Since I couldn't deal with the disparities and was, by disposition, too sunny to move it all to the *Bad* column, I appear to have shifted the whole lot over to the *Good* column.

After all, there was genuine *Good* in the baffling mix. I loved college. I'd walk across the campus quad on the hilltop each year in late October with leaves every shade of red, gold, and brown flitting past my face in cool autumn gusts and, with tears stinging in my eyes, thank God for the privilege of going to college. I knew my parents were paying for it by the skin of their teeth alongside my sorority dues, my drill-team costumes, and my new polyester sweater, pleated wool skirt, and knee-high boots. Mom got a job outside the home for the first time in her life working in women's wear at Craig's, a department store, to help take the edge off the expenses. She told me that, every time she wrote a check for my tuition or Tony's, she prayed with all her might it wouldn't bounce. Ultimately both of us would graduate free of student loans, thanks to our mom and dad. I'm reminded again I should've bought them a car with my first royalty check and feel guilty that it's been a while since I felt guilty over it.

● ● ●

A life-altering moment occurred during my college years that is automatically underwhelming by the sheer telling of it, but everything afterward hinges on it. The summer between my freshman and sophomore years I returned home, got a temporary part-time job at Craig's in the baby department to be near Mom, and threw myself into church at Spring Woods Baptist. Within a few weeks, talk was circulating among the women.

"The sixth-grade girls don't have anyone to go with them to GA camp as a sponsor." GA stood for Girls' Auxiliary, a program in Southern Baptist churches that trained young girls to love missions and pray for missionaries. "All the moms either have jobs or other kids they can't leave."

There was also no air-conditioning, but this was incidental to mature women of God. This was an emergency. Imagine what our girls could become if they missed church camp.

"I don't know if y'all need someone older," I said with a drawl thick as corn-bread batter, "but if an eighteen-year-old can qualify as a sponsor and y'all would trust me with them, I'd—"

A van was packed to the gills with girls, pillows, bedrolls, and bags, gassed up and in drive practically before they knew my last name. We were on our way to Peach Creek Baptist Encampment for five days.

The facilities were simple and standard. Each cabin had about twelve bunk beds. My six girls and I shared the space with a couple of other small groups and their sponsors. I chose a bottom bunk, which gave the girls convenient access for the obligatory shenanigans like toothpaste between my toes and rice between my sheets. Mornings were for gatherings in the open-air pavilion where we'd hear from missionaries, then we'd break into small groups for guided discussions. Afternoons were for swimming (one-pieces only), games, and raiding the snack bar, or for returning to the cabin to rest or write letters to their moms. I wrote to mine, too. Evenings were set aside for a more formal service similar to Sunday morning church, hymn-singing included.

Each night before lights-out, I'd gather my girls around my bottom bunk and give them a bedtime devotional and discuss whatever was on their minds. They'd scoot in close in their paja-mas, and a few of the other girls in the cabin would scrunch up with us. I fell in love with those sixth graders. I gave them every-thing I had, which was admittedly piddling. I shared what I knew about God and taught them during free time how to make use of every hot roller in a jumbo tray. They couldn't get that from just anybody. It took considerable hair.

Come the fourth day of camp, I got up before dawn to jump into the shower before anyone else stirred. I was standing at the sink about to brush my teeth when it happened. Nothing was the least remarkable about the surroundings. They were, in fact, camp-level crude. The bathroom had a couple of commode stalls with typical industrial green metal doors, most of which had relaxed from the hinges so that the sliding bar to lock the door was no longer parallel to the hole. Beside the stalls were several slender showers, each with a plastic cloudy-white curtain hanging from rings and mildewed at the bottom. The floor was painted concrete, cracked and peeling. The wet bathing suits draped over stall doors and hanging from hooks filled the room with the distinct scent of chlorine with a hint of mold.

It was right there at the sink I sensed the Lord's presence. I didn't see anything. I didn't hear anything. No thunder, no heat, no light, no still, small voice. No finger writing in the steam of the mirror facing me. My toothbrush didn't levitate. The hair on my head didn't stand on end. I did not see a vision. I didn't manifest a sudden spiritual gifting or, as I recall, say a word. So bereft was the moment of any tangible sign, I've wished over and over to go back to the time and place and experience it again so I could relive it as a grown-up and put it under a theological microscope. All I have to go on is the conviction of an eighteen-year-old to whom the sense of God's presence was intense enough to make her grip both sides of the sink until the moment passed.

I could have imagined it, but such things were not in my realm of thinking. I'd never heard of anyone having a remotely mystical experience. I feel like I'd have chosen a better venue to drum up a divine visitation than a bathroom where a toilet constantly ran and the showerheads dripped maddeningly. I've got no proof, of course, and really only one thing that testifies to the authenticity of it, and that's the permanence of the effects. In a lifetime of second-guesses, I've never doubted something holy and unique to my experience took place in that most unholy surrounding. Something big enough to become the *before* and *after* on my time-line. On a lifetime roller coaster of failures and successes, losses and gains, revivals, restructures, and reversals, whatever happened that early morning has never let me go or, in the same way, ever been repeated.

"You were filled with the Holy Spirit," a fellow women's ministry leader told me adamantly a couple of years ago, and I was not at all put off by her explanation or her confidence.

"I don't think so," I said. "I hope I've been filled with the Holy Spirit lots of times. I pray for God to fill me with his Spirit every morning of my life, but the moment didn't feel like *filled*. I felt something more like, well, *surrounded*."

"Well, then, what did *you* feel was the point?"

"If I had to come up with a term for something I sensed in my spirit instead of actually hearing or seeing, I'd say it was ownership. Like God conveying in this weird sort of way, *You're mine*. Thing is, I already was. I'm positive I was already in Christ and had been for at least half of my life."

The funny thing about having what you think might have been an encounter with God is how you just go on doing all the earthy things, like getting acid indigestion. I brushed my teeth. I didn't know what else to do. It's why I'd come to the sink in the first place. I whisked up and down the incisors and the canines, back and forth on the molars, then I spit right there in the same sink I'd gripped on account of the holy presence. There's got to be something better to do in the wake of the sacred than spit. The bathroom didn't look or smell any better than it had. The locks on the bathroom stalls still didn't work. I stared for a few seconds into the mirror, tilting my head this way and that. I didn't look any different. I bent down and gathered up my damp towel and my toiletry bag and stepped out of the bathroom, not one whit wiser or better that I could tell. Nothing at all was different . . . yet everything had changed.

The early morning sun was just beginning to beam through the windows on a cabin full of deep-sleeping sixth-grade girls, some of their chins agape, their tonsils nearly showing, one with a strand of her brown hair adhered to the corner of her mouth, their unbathed and disproportionately large feet poking out of their bedrolls, and all of them utterly disheveled and breathtakingly beautiful. My heart melted on the concrete floor like a scoop of lard in my nanny's skillet.

"Morning, sunshines!" I said it good and loud. "This is the day the Lord has made. Somebody better get up, rejoice, and be glad in it!" I'd end up practically dragging them by their long feet off those bunks.

I attended the morning session with my girls like usual, but once I got them settled into their small groups, I made a beeline to the woman overseeing the camp and asked if I could have a word with her. She was gracious and accommodating and listened carefully to what I had to say. "Something weird happened to me this morning."

"I'm all ears," she replied.

I've thought a thousand times how this scenario could have gone. These were days of sharp divides between the charismatic and noncharismatic traditions in Christianity. The woman sitting across from me didn't know me from Eve, and this was a Southern Baptist encampment. How easily she could have discounted my story or feared I was under charismatic influence and discouraged me from ever giving credence to anything vaguely experiential. I'm amazed that, even if she believed what had happened to me was real, she didn't feel duty-bound to discourage me from making too much out of it.

She leaned forward attentively and looked me straight in the eye as I spoke, her legs crossed, her left elbow on her knee, and her chin rested on her palm. The story didn't take me long. The absurdity was how little there was to tell.

When I finished, she dropped her hand from her chin and smoothed the fold in her skirt over her knee and said slowly and directly, "I believe, Beth, that you have received what we Baptists would term *a call to vocational Christian service.*"

I listened pensively, neither nodding nor shaking my head.

"Now, here is what you need to do next."

I've told this part of the story a number of times, hoping that, somewhere along the way, it would reach the woman who sat across from me with her hair slightly teased and pinned up loosely in a French twist, and she'd contact me and I could tell her what fitting counsel she offered me for that moment in time. Of all names for me to leave unrecorded, this key person in my life remains anonymous.

"I want you to go right back to church this coming Sunday . . ."

"Yes, ma'am." I nodded. "I'll be there."

"And, at the end of the service, when your pastor—now, who is your pastor, Beth?"

"Dr. Dean Burke of Spring Woods Baptist in Houston. We call him Brother Burke."

"Okay, when Brother Burke gives the invitation—"

"For people to come forward who want to receive Jesus as Savior or join the church?" I already knew this was what she meant, but this was my vexatious way of letting her know I was following her. That she appeared unvexed was a grace.

"Yes, when Brother Burke gives the invitation for people who are making a decision regarding Jesus, I want you to step out into the aisle—"

"Like I did when I was nine?"

"Is that when you made your profession of faith?" she inquired.

"Yes, ma'am."

"Yes, then. Just like when you were nine, I want you to step out into the aisle and walk straight to your pastor and tell him you believe you have received a call to vocational Christian service. In our denomination, we make this public to our church family just like we made our profession of faith. He will help steer you from there."

● ● ●

That's exactly what I did and, thanks be to God, what my pastor did. Brother Burke warmly received me, invited me to stand alongside several others who'd come forward to join the church, and after introducing them, he shared with the congregation my decision to follow Jesus into vocational service. There I was again, nine years old times two, at the front of a church receiving the right hand of fellowship from a line of people an aisle long.

I know now how awry this could have gone at any point. I

could have told my experience, whatever it may have been, to a ministry leader or pastor and, instead of falling into trustworthy hands, been discredited, shut down, misled, exploited, used or misused. I was a prime candidate to be groomed for abuse.

I couldn't articulate it then, but in retrospect, I know that I'd surrendered to full-time ministry. I had no idea what the ministry was. Not sure what it would yet be. I envied the boys who could confidently say, "God called me to preach!" What on earth was less credible in my world than a girl obsessed with mascara, lip gloss, and hot rollers saying she'd received a vocational calling from God and no clue what to? I hadn't the least notion what a woman in my denomination could do. I supposed I would become a missionary, but even that seemed so far-fetched at the time, I couldn't picture it.

I served at my church all that summer and returned to college in late August. I'd had no further encounter with God in those months nor, strangely, the expectation of one. My spiritual disciplines were nascent and my sanctification woefully underdeveloped, but I kept whittling away at the little I knew to do. I assumed if I were supposed to change my course for college, I'd get some kind of signal, and I never did. I continued pursuing a political science major and a minor in English and threw in a teacher's certificate for good measure.

What happened that morning wouldn't be the last time I'd perceive an unusual move of the Spirit but, to date, never in the same way. Who knows why I've had a smattering of mystical experiences in my walk with God in a tradition rather resistant to them? An individual can go an entire lifetime without feeling anything out of the ordinary and have no less Spirit, no less calling, no less purpose, faith, or gifting, and certainly no less fruitfulness.

He or she will also be considerably less controversial. The less common experiences I've shared along the way have caused more skepticism than credibility, and understandably so. They would be easy to contrive and just as easy to misunderstand, blow out of proportion, or exploit. My experience is not meant to be a standard of any kind. God is sovereign and reserves the right to both order and creativity.

When I let the wind catch the pages of Scripture from Genesis to Revelation, I find nowhere to land on one precise pattern for what it looks like to be summoned by God to walk with him or called by Jesus to follow him. God told Abram, "Go." On the other hand, the voice of the Lord said within the hearing of Isaiah, "Whom shall I send? And who will go for us?" and Isaiah volunteered. "Here am I! Send me!" Jesus said directly to some of his disciples, "Follow me." Others were brought to him by those he'd summoned. All come to Jesus by faith. No one comes by formula.

From where I sit, where I stand, where I walk, where I run, where I rest, where I pray, play, and weep, my story looks like a shirt too long left in the bottom of a clothes hamper. Were I to bleach and launder it, starch and iron it to stand up properly, crisp and straight, it would look a whole lot better, but I am certain of this—it would no longer fit.

CHAPTER TEN

I'D NOTICED HIM BEFORE. He was the kind of handsome hard not to notice. The first time I recall seeing him was across the college cafeteria. I was seated at a long table with friends from drill team, finishing up a fast meal before an all-evening practice. We were so accustomed to the roar of trays clattering, plates clanging, and students chattering, we thought nothing of having to yell to be heard at the table.

"Miracle Whip."

"What'd you say, Beth?"

"Miracle Whip!" I said a second time, employing the full use of my lungs.

"What about it?"

"I don't understand it!"

"What don't you understand about Miracle Whip?"

Meaningless conversations can be the truest test of good friendships. Anyone can talk about the heavy stuff.

"I don't understand why even a college cafeteria wouldn't know you can't put anything but real mayonnaise in blue cheese dressing," I railed. "Why even bother? Why not just accept your mediocrity and serve Thousand Island?"

The few listening studied the triangles of milky iceberg lettuce dripping on the ends of their forks. Salad was the safest thing to eat before practice if we wanted to keep our supper down for two hours of high kicks. No one could tell us the football players practiced harder than we did. We knew they'd have cried like babies after the first hour of Mrs. Tidwell hollering, "Again!" with two long *a*'s. Any one of us on the squad could have kicked a superior field goal. At least the football players got to really eat.

"I don't even like blue cheese dressing," one of them chirped.

"That's because you've only eaten it with Miracle Whip!"

This was about the time I saw him walk into the cafeteria wearing a Western shirt, Wrangler jeans, and cowboy boots, looking a lot like a young George Strait, and I momentarily lost my train of thought.

"Mean Green, we gotta go!"

These were the peak years of fame for Mean Joe Greene, a Texas boy who first sparked a twinkle in the eye of sports fans as a defensive player for the University of North Texas Mean Green football team, then shot off like a rocket to Pittsburgh to play for the Steelers. A friend had an enamel pin bearing the words *Mean Green* and latched it on the lapel of my drill team cape one day and it stuck. It was a natural nickname for anyone with my last name, and I liked it because I'd been told I could be irritatingly cheerful. They'd never seen me get worked up over Miracle Whip.

I was still wondering if the guy who'd made it to the meat and

potato line by now was new to campus and, if not, how I'd managed to miss those boots, when I realized my friends were halfway
out the cafeteria door, capes whipping in the wind. I jumped up,
pitched my tray on the conveyor belt, and darted to catch up
with them.

The next time I saw the guy from the cafeteria was about a
month into the semester. My little brother, Tony, had joined me
at Southwest Texas State that year, when I was a junior and he was
a freshman. We planned to meet in a parking lot on campus one
afternoon to run an errand together. Tony was in the middle of a
conversation with someone whose back was to me when I walked
up. When Tony saw me, he said, "Hey, Keith, this is my big sister,
Beth." He turned to me. "Beth, I met Keith at a fraternity rush
party. He's president of the Pikes. Keith, Beth's president of Chi
Omega. Maybe y'all have met." We shook our heads *no* and said
the proper *nice-to-meet-yous*. We were both in relationships with
other people at this point and neither one of us gave away any
signs of interest. We simply took note.

Five days later, I walked into the two-bedroom apartment I
shared with three of my friends and there he was, standing in
our den, this time in a polo shirt and Wrangler jeans. Two of my
apartment mates were "little sisters" to his fraternity, meaning they
knew one another well, and he'd stopped by to say hi. Fact was,
though I was in and out of the room for the next fifteen minutes,
he said hi to everybody *but* me, which was precisely how I began
to suspect he'd come to see me. There is a way between a man and
a woman who keep one another in the corner of their eye.

When Keith left, I gave him time to descend one flight of stairs,
then opened the door, leaned over the rail, and said, "Hey!"

He looked up sheepishly then glanced right and left. "Are you
talking to me?"

"Yes! Just wanted to say, next time you're in our apartment seeing your friends, you can actually talk to me, too."

He flashed a smile and his face flushed red. "Okay, then. *I will.*"

I grinned, then stepped back through my apartment door and shut it. We continued turning up, unplanned, in the same places, like a puppeteer was holding two sets of strings.

The next date on our sorority's fall schedule, and one long-since set, was a mixer at the Pike house with his fraternity. Rest assured, I have exactly zero interest in writing about Greek life on a college campus unless it is New Testament Greek, but alas, it has an unavoidable place in my story. About an hour into the party, Keith walked across the spacious room toward me and shouted over Fleetwood Mac crooning "Go Your Own Way." "May I grab you a beer?"

"No, thank you!"

He appeared a tad thrown by my response. Thinking maybe I was too highbrow for a beer, he tried a different beverage. "How about a margarita?"

I shook my head. "Thank you, though!"

"A piña colada?" This being a keg party with paper cups, I felt this was a reach.

I shouted back, "Thanks anyway. The thing is—" Oblivious to the last note of "Go Your Own Way," I picked that one silent moment to yell at the top of my lungs, "I don't drink!"

I didn't have to worry about whether the fraternity president standing five feet in front of me heard what I said. From the look on his face, cute as he was, he clearly had no place in his twenty-one-year-old brain to file this piece of data. Flummoxed, he turned around and started walking off as the next record blasted over the sound system.

"But I dance," I yelled.

In what, to this day, is perhaps the single most romantic gesture I've ever been privy to receive, the young man with the mysterious redwood eyes and hair the shade of a moonless midnight spun around, stretched out his arm, opened his palm, and said, "Well, then. May I have this dance?"

• • •

By the time we each knew how deeply troubled the other was, it was too late. We were a guy and a girl with next to nothing but chronic brokenness in common, too lovestruck to take our differences seriously. Our variances spanned the spectrum: theological, ideological, political, financial, familial. Keith was a deer hunter. I thought hunting was barbaric. I loved poetry. He'd burst out laughing by the third rhyme. His family had new money and fine cars. My family was deep in debt, and the left taillight on my dad's overwrought Cadillac was duct-taped to the bumper. Keith cussed like he was born for it, and I spoke fluent Christian cheese. I thought he'd grow out of it. He thought I would.

Both our families unapologetically preferred our previous love interests. We had all the support of a house of cards. Like most wounded people, Keith and I brought out the worst in one another. Any relationship counselor worth ten dollars in compensation would have declared us humanly incompatible and been exactly right.

Isn't that the way it is? We think we can break all the rules and still be the exceptions who make it. We think love will always be enough, but when we're early in it and the chemistry is acute, we don't know that love isn't always a feeling. We haven't yet learned it is as often an action when we're momentarily bankrupt of affection.

I've reflected no few times, as Keith surely has, on how much easier our lives could have been if we'd made sure we were genuine friends with common interests and not just two matchsticks living in unfettered friction, about to burn one another to the ground. Then again, I always end up wondering if, for us, it had to be this way. I wonder if God has had his way in this untamable whirlwind and storm. I wonder if the extraordinary difficulty was essential to the shaping of our clay, and not solely the consequence of our compromised hearts.

At least we lived in the same city. Keith was a fourth-generation Houstonian. His bloodline reaches back to the hallowed days when Texas was a Republic. Anyone who finds little meaning in this was brought into this world, as I was, in one of the lesser forty-nine. Real Texans are born here. Real Texans stay here—or if some cruel twist of fate downgrades them elsewhere, they are compelled by some immutable pledge sewn deep in their lone-starred hearts to testify to their Texasness in under ninety seconds per encounter. They may be mannerly enough to do it subtly ("Thank you for helping me since I don't know my way around here because, well, you see, I'm from Texas"), but they will do it. They cannot help themselves. Texas is a hot oven where certain ingredients are baked in. I do not write these words without appreciation. I simply speak verifiable facts that may be tested and tried.

Keith came from hardworking blue-collar stock. One grandfather and several uncles managed to strike gold unstopping Houston's toilets, but it's fair to say his dad outdid them all. His name was doubly painted on the sides of white plumbing vans all over the metroplex. The slogan read, "Call John and get Moore!" Beneath it, the company name: John Moore Plumbing. Handsome, rugged, and magnetic, the man gave the whole industry dignity, managing to pull up the collective pants of Houston's plumbers.

One of the earliest times I went to the Moores' house, Keith said he was starving and did I want a sandwich. No, I said, but followed him into the kitchen lest I be left alone with his family members glaring at me with the side-eye. He grabbed a loaf of bread, unwound the twist tie, and drew out two pieces of thick-sliced and slapped them on the kitchen island, all the while talking about the time he accidentally nailed himself to the back fence. He opened the double-wide refrigerator, pulling a package of sliced ham out of the meat compartment and a beefsteak tomato from the veggie drawer. He reached back in the refrigerator one last time, and that's when it happened. He withdrew his rugged tan fist from the deluxe Frigidaire with a fifteen-ounce jar of Miracle Whip in it. I commenced to having never seen one human being so generous of hand with a condiment in my life.

"Keith, you like Thousand Island, don't you?"

"Yeah, why?"

We fought over Miracle Whip versus real mayonnaise all the way back to my house, neither one of us giving an inch.

● ● ●

We fought about everything. Everything but one thing. We were already getting along poorly enough that I figured we'd marry. He knew I was serious about my faith, but we hadn't had "the talk," and I was getting nervous. We were back in San Marcos for our spring semester. There was this big rock not far from my apartment, and he'd picked me up and set me on top of it and we were flirting the way a young man and woman in love will do.

"Keith, I need to tell you something."

"What?" he said and kissed me on the hand.

"I'm serious. I need you to know something."

"Tell me," he said, now kissing my fingertips.

"Keith! Look me in the eye!" And he did. "Keith, I need you to know I'm gonna work for God."

He looked a bit stupefied. "What do you mean?"

"I mean," I said intensely, "I'm going to work for God. Like, all my life."

I wouldn't say he dropped my hand like a hot potato, exactly, but close. "How do you know?"

"He told me I was going to."

"God told you that you were going to work for him."

"Yes, Keith. But not with words. With a knowing. Do you know what I mean by *a knowing*?" Good grief, I hardly knew what I meant by *a knowing*. Most people I knew didn't even believe in *a knowing*.

His dark brows drew down nearly to his thick eyelashes. "What are you going to do?"

"I have no idea." My stomach flipped. This had gone better with Brother Burke.

"So, let me see if I have this straight. God told you that you were going to work for him."

"Yes."

"But he did not tell you what you were going to do."

"Yes. Well, I mean, no, he didn't tell me what I was going to do."

Keith put his hands on his hips and stared so hard into my eyes, I thought he'd bore a hole through my pupils to the back side of my skull. "Let me ask you something."

"Okay," I replied, starting to feel a little nauseous.

"You gonna be a nun?" With his Catholic background, it was the only thing he could imagine an overly zealous religious girl doing.

"No!" I shouted, incredulous on account of the way we'd been kissing for the last half hour.

"Well, in that case, I can live with it."

And he did. And he has. And God knows neither of us could have imagined what was coming.

We tied the knot on the thirtieth of the next December in a low-budget ceremony that was fine by me. I wore an appropriately off-white wedding dress we'd rented for sixty dollars. Most of them were fifty, but Mom and I went for broke.

"You're the only person I'd marry at the peak of deer season," Keith told me emphatically.

Well over forty years ago we said our vows in front of our guests and two families, the latter of whom looked like they'd mistaken a wedding for a funeral. Over time, we each grew on the other's family. We just didn't get in a hurry about it. Mom never took down the family picture my previous boyfriend was in, she loved him so, but she did finally cut Keith's face out of a snapshot and glue it over Scott's. Since Keith looked all right in Scott's suit, I accepted it. Marriage has everything to do with acceptance, I think.

Keith's only been home for a half dozen or so of our wedding anniversaries due to deer season. We celebrate it. We just celebrate it late. I never really mind. Making it another year for Keith and me has mostly been about God and each of us individually, anyway.

127

CHAPTER ELEVEN

A FEW NIGHTS AFTER WE GOT BACK from a weeklong honeymoon cruise in the Caribbean, I awakened out of a dead sleep to Keith standing straight up on our bed, shouting at the top of his lungs. I bolted off the mattress and scanned the room for an intruder. We were the only ones there. I pulled the short chain on the bedside table lamp and looked at my young husband, who was wild-eyed and terrified and clearly seeing something I couldn't.

"Baby, it's me," I said, reaching toward him gingerly, unsure he was safe to touch. "I think you've had a bad dream."

Keith glanced my way with a measure of recognition. I was sure once he realized it was me, I wouldn't be in danger. He was a mysterious guy. A brooder to be sure, but if I knew anything about him at all, I knew he loved me. Nearly worshiped me. I knew in my gut he wouldn't physically harm me on purpose. His arms were still stiff, the veins bulging, and his fists clenched, but his gaze was now flashing back and forth between me and whatever he saw in front of him.

I touched his hand. "Ivan, baby." His first name and what, nearly from the start, I've always called him. "It's me. I'm right here. Let's sit down on the bed. Are you with me here? Can you hear me?"

He nodded. I tugged on his hand to urge him downward. He complied but sat as stiff as he'd stood.

I rubbed his back gently. "You've had a bad dream is all." *Dear Jesus, let that be all.* "We're safe, honey, we're safe," I whispered. "Want me to get you some water?"

He nodded.

I headed to the kitchen, weak-kneed and wobbly, my mind whirling, and filled a plastic glass with tap water. We both held the glass steady while he took a few sips. He made some sounds, groans mostly, but never said a word.

"Lie back down, honey. It's over now. All is well." *Dear Jesus, let it be over now. Let all be well.*

He lay back, his head on one edge of the pillow, then turned away from me on his side and fell back to sleep, if indeed he'd ever been awake. My heart banged in my chest like a boot trying to kick down a door. Such was my jarring introduction to what would become commonly known as post-traumatic stress disorder.

Boy, had Keith earned it.

Funeral services for Marcel John Moore III, 3, son of Mr. and Mrs. M. J. Moore, Jr., . . . will be held at 9:30 a.m. Monday at St. Theresa's Catholic Church. Burial will be in the Garden of Gethsemane. The boy

died Friday night of injuries received in an explosion at
his home last Sunday.

THE HOUSTON POST

They were little more than toddlers, Keith and his big brother,
"Duke," the elder as towheaded as the younger was dark. They
were playing in the attached garage of their small home, happy as
could be, and thought to gas up their tiny plastic lawn mower with
the orange can their daddy used for the big one. The fuel gurgled
and splashed from the can to the toy, and it then rolled mercilessly
underneath the water heater bearing a slender blue flame. Duke
got the worst of it since his clothes were doused. Keith's physical
body bore fewer burns, but his tender two-year-old mind sustained blisters too broad and deep to soothe and bandage. Both
boys were rushed by ambulances to the nearest hospital and placed
in the same room. Duke was in and out; Keith never lost con-
sciousness. I am told he never stopped screaming. He'd recall one
particular image. *Brother . . . wrapped in cotton balls.*

"Burial will be in the Garden of Gethsemane."

The place of pleading and pores bleeding. That place where
you enter in with Jesus and crawl on your hands and knees and
fall on your face before God, begging for the cup of suffering to
pass by you, but the chalice is so close to you now and the moon
so full, you can see your reflection in the gold. Your face is con-
torted with dread, the whites of your eyes luminous with horror.
Not everyone comes out.

"Burial will be in the Garden of Gethsemane."

Burial in the dirt you dug up bruising your knees, begging. It
is the place where those who believe come at their rawest, skinless
and vulnerable, powerless, helplessly dependent, thrown at the
mercy of a God they hope is listening. It is there a petitioner sobs,

"I won't live through this if this cup doesn't pass. Do what you're going to do, God, do your will, do it above my own because you alone are God. But know that I cannot, will not, come out of this alive." Keith and his mom got buried there with Duke in the Garden of Gethsemane, the one in cotton swaddling clothes, freed from his pain and made whole in the presence of God, cuddled and unafraid and set down, his blond hair tousled by the hand of God, and loosed to play. The other two of them were buried alive. There would be no play. Others in the family grieved, but these two would never recover.

Gethsemane is all the things we fear most except one. We fear we are unheard. We're sure of it, but it is not true. It was in that original Gethsemane that Jesus, in the words of Hebrews 5:7, "offered prayers and appeals with loud cries and tears to the one who was able to save him from death, and he was heard . . ."

And we are heard.

•   •   •

Keith's instability had nothing on mine. We entered marriage equally troubled. Equally proficient at hiding our harms until we were exposed to the fluorescent floodlight of life under a shared roof. Two years after we married, he'd lose his younger sister in a day's time to a catastrophic brain aneurysm. I asked my mother-in-law once how she ever survived such losses.

"I didn't mean to," she replied, and I knew she meant it. "I just kept waking up."

Sometimes you wake up when you don't even want to. But maybe God keeps you waking up till one day, many days later, you grow a little gladder that you did.

Over the slow crawl of some long and challenging years, the

sharp edges of the fractures I'd sustained in childhood dulled just enough to allow me to generally flourish. Keith's fractures came at the hand of such savage instruments that he steps on shards nearly every step he takes. He told me once, "Lizabeth, life is harder for some people than others."

I wanted to argue with him. I wanted to say how everyone had the same opportunity to be happy in Jesus. I wanted to ask him why the blessings of the present couldn't make up for the curses of the past. I wanted to ask him why I wasn't enough to make him too glad to be sad, but I knew I'd be talking like a fool. Life *is* harder for some people than others. Shadows follow me often enough, but not incessantly. Not everywhere I go. I've not spent a single night's sleep in a burning garage. I deal with bouts of anxiety and depression, but they don't chase me down constantly like ravenous wolves after a bleating sheep. I wondered sometimes, as most kids do, if my parents really loved me, but never once was I faced with circumstances wooing me to wonder if my parents wished their other child had been the one to survive.

Solomon said a long time ago in Proverbs 14:10 that "each heart knows its own bitterness" (NIV), and I think he was on to something. No other human can climb down our throats like a spelunker and hack through our trachea and try on our hearts and see how they feel. One mortal cannot fully comprehend how another operates from within. Jesus is the only outsider who truly knows the insider our skin keeps veiled. Look the world over for two people with identical afflictions, injuries, infirmities, regrets, losses, tragedies, and missed opportunities, and if by some anomaly you find them, they still won't have the same DNA, background, living conditions, physical conditions, and support systems to navigate them with.

"Each heart knows its own bitterness."

Two wounds could require the same number of stitches, yet cause varied levels of pain. Not all stage 4 cancers are alike, nor are the hearts, minds, and bodies dealing with them. No two head-on collisions have identical ramifications. We are distinct whether we want to be or not. Even of marriage, the Lord said the two shall become one flesh. He did not say we'd become one heart. He did not say we'd become one mind.

● ● ●

Keith would ultimately be diagnosed not only with severe PTSD but also with bipolar disorder. I stare at those last two words because this is the first I've written them for public consumption. I asked my man while I was writing this memoir, "Shall we tell our real story or not? It's up to you. I won't tell anything you're not comfortable with. But we're in our sixties now, honey. Some couple, some family, some reader we'd never otherwise reach might need to hear our story."

Keith stood in front of me with his hands on his hips, head tilted, eyes locked with mine. "You thinking details?"

"Nope," I said, and I wasn't.

"Will you leave out—?"

I didn't let him finish. "I'll leave out anything you want. This is your call. You draw the line." I've come to believe that, far beyond the more romantic things, love means finding some measure of safety with one another in a world that couldn't be less safe. Silence.

"Let's do it, then," he finally replied.

What every author hopes but has no right nor power to demand is that the reader will deal gently with records of sacred things. Vulnerability, in and of itself, is sacred because it mirrors, if even in a glass darkly, the image of Christ. Pulling the bandage back and giving someone a glimpse of a wound that, in this life, will likely never fully heal but only hope to be treated, is *expensive*.

The conundrum is that we cannot know what it will cost until it's too late and already shown. What we do want and hope and pray—Keith and I—is to offer somebody lonely a little company. We have been lonely. We have felt unknown. We've felt like people in our social stratospheres could not understand why we cannot always do the things they do, go the places they go, count on the things they count on. We can't always plan. We can no more fix another individual's similar challenges than we can fix our own, but we can help another feel less alone. We can stand with another family in spirit and nod. "Yes, we get it. Yes, we've felt that. Yes, we feared that."

We've had a hard go, my guy and I. Life can be mean. Mental illness is mean. It can be heartless to the one it needles and harasses, and hateful to the ones nearby. Mental illness may be a lot of things, but there is at least one thing it is not. It is not someone's fault. Keith and I have gone through agonizing situations of our own making, our own foolishness, selfishness, and sinfulness. The most relentless winds that have battered our four walls for decades on end, beaten our windowpanes with frozen rain, whistled through the cracks in our doors, and threatened to blow our house down, however, are outside our doing. Outside our causing. Outside our fixing.

For us and for so many others like us, what works beautifully— nearly magically—more often than not works only for a while. More ups, more downs. More tears. More conflicts. More appointments. More blood tests. *Let's raise this, lower this, discontinue this, start this.* More exhaustion. More pulling our hair out. More holding hands. More trying again. More fighting the urge to not try again . . .

We've had a hard go, yes, but we've also had, by the grace of God, divine consolations and—at each of our bests—mutual compassion. Commitment, sometimes just one of us at a time till it's both of us again. What we have had, by the grace of God, is courage to seek help again, and again, and again, and again. What we have had, by the grace of God, are some good friends we finally trusted enough to tell. What *I* have had, by the grace of God, is a man willing to submit to doctors' orders, willing to do what it takes to live under a continuous medical protocol that is constantly, maddeningly changing. These are not small things. These are to the tremendous credit of Keith Moore.

CHAPTER TWELVE

"MARRIAGE HAS MADE ME SICK."

I say these words to my mother while sitting in her small breakfast room in Houston two months after my wedding day. We're sipping percolated Folgers out of china teacups. She's thawed out a Sara Lee cheesecake and cut us each a tiny sliver. She has a knack for assuming nobody's very hungry. She sets them on the saucers meant for the china teacups. She opens a can of cherry pie filling and puts a teaspoonful on each of our pieces. Mine is still a little frozen in the middle, but can the chronically ill even care?

"What kind of sick?"

She pushes her saucer back and reaches for a cigarette and her ashtray to prepare herself for my response. I'd like to have a smoke myself, but I don't. Too dizzy, and anyway, I need a divorce because marriage has made me sick.

"I'm so tired I can hardly lift my little finger."

"Honey, you should have told me this sooner. What else?" Mom wasn't much of a toucher, but she could really love a person with her eyes. She loves me deeply. I can see it on her face. I can smell it in her coffee. I can taste it in her cheesecake.

"I'm constantly sick to my stomach."

"I see," she says, eyes narrowing.

"It's gotten so bad, I've started throwing up every day. I shouldn't have married him."

"Tell me what else, honey," she says. I've got her full attention.

I hear the clock on the mantel strike 5 p.m. I'll have to go home soon. I don't make a habit of talking to my mother about intimate matters, but I clearly have a cancer of some kind and this is no time for timidity. "Mom—" I look away on this part out of embarrassment—"my breasts are so sore that I can hardly stand it."

"Both of them?"

"Yes! Sore all the way under my arms." I choke up. It sounds even worse now that I've spoken the bad news into the atmosphere. Here I am, just twenty-one. I'm wondering if I'm underage enough to get an annulment.

She puts out her cigarette, halfway smoked, so I sit straight up.

"Bethie," she says in such a way that I look right at her, "you're not sick." Denial is rife in my family.

"Yes, Mom! I am!"

"No, honey, you're not. You're pregnant." And she grins a grin as marvelous and mischievous as any I'd ever see stretch across her face.

Let the reader who wonders how I could possibly have been so ignorant understand that I'd been recently diagnosed with a badly tilted uterus and such severe endometriosis that I'd been assured of the need for surgery to conceive. Let the reader also understand that such assurances can be faulty.

●　●　●

The nurse peeked her head through my hospital room door around four in the morning. "Mrs. Moore, you awake?"

"Yes, ma'am."

I'd shut my eyes for an hour or so, exhausted and weak in a way I'd never known, but I hadn't managed to fall asleep. My mind kept trying to catch up with what my body had been through.

The nurse's name was Marianne. I know because I journaled it. No one warns you how bonded you're going to feel to the nurses who walked with you, as my nanny and mom would say, through the valley of the shadow. You think the nurses feel the same bond, and that they'll quit their job and go home with you from the hospital, crowded in the back seat with the flower vases and the baby, and take care of you both for weeks—or maybe even till kindergarten—because you're both so special.

They won't mind doing this free of charge either. You can see the future plain as day: your OB-GYN nurse right next to you at the baby's high school graduation.

Marianne didn't hit the light switch, but from the interminable level of fluorescent wattage in the hallway spilling into my room, I could see the front of a bassinet cart in the doorway. "I bet I have something you want," she chirped.

"You do! You surely do!" I replied, scooting up the bed and into a sitting position, wincing. The nurse rolled the bassinet to the left side of my bed, scooped up its passenger, and placed her in my arms.

"Thank you," I whispered.

"You're welcome, honey. How ya feelin'?"

"Good right this second."

"Hit the call button when you need some help. I'm about to go off the clock, but you'll be in good hands." She shut the door behind her.

This was the first chance the baby and I had gotten to be alone. She had been born at exactly 5:18 p.m. the evening before, weighing in at seven pounds and three ounces. A half hour later, according to my journal, Keith announced her arrival to twenty-five people to be precise. All of them exuberantly endured until I was moved to my own room, at which point they all crowded into the small space for an impromptu celebration and prayer meeting. I cased the room, studying the faces of some of the dearest people in the world to us, and knew we were so lucky to be so loved. Come 9 p.m., however, some of us were ready to be less lucky and a smidge less loved, including a newborn passed around like a football and a new mom who couldn't say no.

After all, the day had started before dawn.

Early Sunday morning, I wrote to my firstborn in her baby book, *I felt that it might be getting close to time for your precious birth.*

What I meant by this was that I awakened around five in the morning to the sensation of a small buffalo in my belly, trying to find a way out of my body with its hooves.

I awoke your father at 8:15 and he was ecstatic! I was too afraid to be sure I was in labor, so your father and I prayed about it and the Lord sent us on to church.

I need not trouble my memory. I'm 100 percent certain only one person was doing that particular praying: the same one doing the sending. Keith complied because he knew even less about childbearing than I did. I could end this memoir after the next line inscribed in the baby book because it's really all you need to know.

I taught Sunday school that morning and was in the hospital by 12:35!

I hadn't studied my Sunday school quarterly for nothing. I had sixth graders to teach—and look at the street corners if you want to know what happens to sixth graders who hadn't been in their quarterlies. Not on my watch. I can't say it was pleasant. I taught for forty-five minutes while rocking back and forth on a backless stool like I was meek and humble and riding on a donkey. I brought the lesson to a close without inviting the girls to share prayer requests, which normally was my favorite part. Based on this practice alone, I was confident I knew more about the personal lives of our congregants than the pastor, and what could be more rewarding besides giving birth right there on the linoleum in a Sunday school room?

I found Keith posthaste and suggested we might consider on this occasion forgoing the worship service and, instead, run by our house, grab my bags and head on over to the hospital. Nothing is close in Houston, Texas. By the time we'd driven the first twenty minutes, I was clocking my contractions at two minutes apart. I grew increasingly anxious.

"Honey, I think you better speed up."

A few minutes passed. "What I mean by speeding up is *step on it.*"

Several more minutes. "For the love of God, if you stop at one more light, I'm going to smack you in the face with this diaper bag."

Don't push. Don't push. Stay in control. I pressed my hand on the dashboard and regulated my breathing like they taught us in Lamaze class. *Definitely in transition,* I told myself. It goes without saying that I'd chosen the self-sacrificing path of natural child-birth. I was strong and well-prepared, and why start your child's life on drugs? (This is as good a time as any to interject that my second child would indeed start her life on drugs.)

Keith wheeled the car up to the hospital emergency room entrance, ran inside to let them know I was advancing quickly, and came back to get me. They hurried me to labor and delivery and had me change into a gown. After performing the exam, Nurse Jean looked at me with her mean, steely eyes.

"Mrs. Moore, you are at two centimeters."

I discerned a judgmental spirit. What Nurse Jean discerned was that I had the longest day of my life ahead of me. Who knew a human could endure that kind of sheer agony and live to tell it?

"Mrs. Moore, are you sure you don't want something to take the edge off?" It should go without saying this was not Nurse Jean.

"I'm sure."

I lied. The only thing I was sure about at this point was that nothing was vaguely natural about childbirth. I'd clutch one of Keith's hands until it was numb and bloodless, then he'd offer me the other. Apart from answering questions, I never made a peep. I'd like to go on record having almost made it. I was down the stretch, trying my best to bear down, when my doctor announced a change of plans.

"Mrs. Moore, we're going to have to give you a saddle block. The little fellow is stuck and we're going to need to help him out, okay?"

He and both nurses were glancing toward the monitor. He was tapping a number with the tip of an index finger inside an indigo glove.

Early that afternoon the nurses had predicted from the heart-beat that the baby was a boy. I already knew it on account of Mom swinging my wedding ring on a chain over my belly a few weeks earlier. "It's a boy," she'd declared with an enthusiasm I could've sworn was a bit forced. Keith and I assumed it all along. Nothing about Keith engendered my confidence in his ability to produce a girl. We'd name him Matthew Keith.

"Mrs. Moore, we need you to sit up a little more. Focus with us."

I nodded my head, swallowing to dampen a blaze of panic scorching my throat. "Will he be all right?" To be sure, they murmured yeses, but the sound was lost in the speed of movement. Nurses were in and out. The lamp was rearranged. Instruments were brought in on a tray. Keith backed up against the wall, looking fifteen years old and lost.

"Beth," the doctor was calling me by my first name now, "on your next contraction, I'm going to insert a needle into your lower back." What he meant was *spine*. "Jean and Marianne are going to lean you forward and hold you really still, but you do your best not to move, too, okay?"

"Yessir." I willed my shaking body as still as possible. I felt the chill of the air conditioner against my bare back. The contraction came in seconds and, with it, the needle. I don't know if I heard the gurgle or simply felt it.

"Good job," he said. "Let's get this baby out."

By the time they repositioned me for delivery, I could no longer feel my legs. A drape was placed over me. Then I heard what sounded like scissors cutting through thick fabric, just once, and watched Keith's face drain to white.

"Beth." The doctor again. "You're going to feel like I'm nearly pulling you off the table, but we've got you. You ready?"

It happened just like he said. I was sure he'd not only gone for the baby but for my liver, my kidneys, and both lungs. After no small commotion, the tone in the room lightened, and Nurse Jean flashed a smile.

"Well, look what we have here. Mr. and Mrs. Moore, you have a daughter."

"A *girl*?" we said, almost in unison, stunned but by no means disappointed.

The drape was removed like a curtain coming up, and a little human fetched from my own body was placed on my chest. The doctor would take the next fifteen minutes to sew me back together again.

The hour that followed was a blur. What I remember most was how deliriously happy my mom was that we'd had a girl. Mind you, she loved boys. She just hadn't had her fill of females yet.

"I'm saying, honey, she's far more alert than the other babies in the nursery. Looking around like she knows exactly what's happening. Like she's wise."

I smiled to see Mom smile and did my best to answer and enter into the wonder, but what I wanted to say to somebody in charge was, "What just happened?" I'd heard of women having babies under shade trees like it was just another day. *Oh, I'll be right back. I'm just gonna go over there and birth a human. Somebody boil water for tea.* The exact word my Lamaze coach had used for pain in childbearing was *manageable*. I was thinking how she better pray she never runs into me at the Walmart.

As an attendant wheeled me out of recovery, I asked for my cosmetics bag and touched up my makeup and instantly assumed the role of cheerful host to that horde of wonderful people in my hospital room. After they filed out, a few at a time, until no one remained but us, my young weary husband took off his boots, lowered the rail on the hospital bed, and crawled in beside me.

"Babe, babe, careful with my IV!"

I could see the surgical tape tugging and the inserted needle lifting the skin on the top of my hand. Keith has a host of marvelous qualities, like loving and affectionate and romantic, but I've yet to hear a single tongue list *gentle* among them. Once I unwound the IV tube from his neck, I folded into his side, glad and grateful to have him next to me. We got to have our newborn for a while, then talked until we were no longer coherent.

When he began to wheeze the way a man falling into deep sleep will do, I nudged him. "Honey, go on home and get in bed and have a night's rest. If you stay any later, I'll be scared to death you'll fall asleep at the wheel."

He kissed me good night and told me what a good job I'd done. He'd see me tomorrow.

I'd been alone a couple of hours when Nurse Marianne rolled the infant carrier in, placed the newborn in my arms, and left the two of us to it. I gave the chain on the overhead lamp one short tug so the room would stay dim. My daughter was wrapped round and round in a thin white blanket, a baby-faced chrysalis. I kissed her tiny cheek, then placed her on my lap and began to unwind the thick dressing. Mom was right. She was surprisingly alert, studious almost, her eyes fixed on my face.

Beneath the layers was Baby Girl Moore in a tiny white diaper, a crisscross undershirt, and a pale-pink boggin cap.

I took the cap off carefully and grimaced at the specks of blood on the inside of it. The baby had a bright-red welt on the back of her head that would turn a deep, mushy purple and a couple of tiny cuts not yet scabbed over. These were signatures of the forceps used to fetch her. She, too, had been through the valley of the shadow, entering this arctic world feeling like someone was trying to behead her.

The thing about life is that, for most folks, it hurts from the start.

She was the most magnificent little creature I'd ever held. I'd held a lot of babies. I loved baby dolls and babies from the time I could toddle. I started babysitting at twelve and, at fourteen, cared for a three- to five-month-old most every weekday of an Arkansas summer in a mobile home while the baby's mom went back to work to support them. I'd helped in the church nursery innumerable times. Nanny used to say of her side of the family tree, "We folk are drunk on babies." I inherited that intoxication in a line of bar shots.

Still, this was different. This baby birthed something in my heart. Something involuntary. Something that had gestated for twenty-two years. I had to have felt that hidden life kick inside my heart at times, but it was now delivered abruptly and reciprocally and irreversibly into the open air. This baby had come for my heart. Welted it front and back. Tore it wide open and brought it out—vulnerable, naked, nicked bloody and blue—into the wind, sunshine, and fury of this world. I'd only feel this frighteningly overtaken with one other infant.

What a pure thing. What an inexplicably pure thing. I'd never felt pure in my life that I could remember, but this little thing squinting her gray-blue eyes back at me, this precious little creature, was the embodiment of innocence. How two such impure people could come up with something like this was unfathomable.

"Hi there, little one. My name is Mom." One tear dropped from my jaw to her tummy, then another. "Your name is Amanda. Aren't you the sweetest little thing?"

It's shocking what a stranger a newborn can be to the very woman who grew and birthed it. You thought he or she would be completely recognizable, utterly familiar and known by you.

A piece of you. The same as you. But you know when you see them—or at least I knew when I saw her—that a much bigger marvel has taken place. The child that grew inside of you and was nourished, protected, and hidden by you is an individual, cut apart from you now, unique from you, moving free of you, seeing the world in a different way from you.

They say newborns can't yet focus, and I'll not suggest this one could. Maybe I was all shades and shadows and all that held her gaze were the sounds. I'm not sure how long I sat with her on my lap, studying her and asking her to tell me about herself. Finally, she stretched, crinkling her forehead, bowing up her whole body and straightening her arms over her head, her hands in fists the size of ten-cent gumballs. I delighted in the way she threw her entire self into it. I had never been so happy in my life. As she finished off the yawn, her chin quivered.

I whispered, "Oh, I'm so sorry. Let's warm you back up." I gathered the blanket back around her and slipped her boggin cap back on her head and held her close, just under my chin.

You were my lifelong dream come true, I'd write a few days later in her baby book. And she was.

●   ●   ●

A little less than three years later, I'd sit in another hospital bed with a second child. Though the anesthesia didn't work nearly as well as promised, both of us made it through labor and delivery with decidedly less trauma and no big scissors. Keith and I mention from time to time how badly we'd wanted a son the second time around, shuddering to imagine what we'd have missed had God not ignored our prayers. It's not that we're partial to girls. It's that we are partial to these girls. These exact two. We named our second Melissa, so she'd go perfectly with Amanda. Three syllables with an accent on the second. Strong *m*'s. Both ending in *a*'s.

They favored one another, except for hair color. Amanda was sunshine blonde. Melissa's hair would lighten for a few years, but she came into this world the same way she ended up: dark-headed. Aside from being equally affectionate and loving throughout, they began and remain as different from one another as two humans from the same couple could be. Most parents of two would say the same, but we emphasize it like a rarity because the distinctions never cease to be astonishing. Amanda was agreeable and eager to please. The way Melissa saw it, nothing could clear the air like a good argument. Amanda's favorite question was "How?" Melissa's, "Why?" Amanda loved books. Peace and stillness. Melissa loved motion. Action. Adventure. Amanda talked at nine and a half months. Melissa walked. Amanda loved long bedtime stories. Melissa, exhausted by each day's end, was asleep before her face landed on the pillowcase. Amanda loved to go on walks. Melissa wanted wheels. Amanda loved horses. Melissa loved Camaros. Amanda was a mama's girl. Melissa was a daddy's girl.

They were both *our* girls.

If Keith had the patience and inclination for an ink pen, he could tell you how he's felt about these two girls. He could count to you how many times he's said he wouldn't trade them for ten sons. He'd boast about how smart and lovely they are, and he'd tell you that nothing makes the four of us collectively happier than making a Moore sandwich. It's nothing original. Just a group hug—Keith and I, two slices of bread; the girls, the peanut butter and jelly. The ham and cheese. Pastrami and Swiss on two slices of rye. Lots of squeezing. Kisses on the cheeks.

Regular stuff, but Keith and I are such irregular people that regular things are remarkable to us. Keith would tell you, if he had you at our table for fried speckled trout he'd caught that morning and macaroni and cheese he made from scratch, what being Dad to little girls has meant to him. Our lives together have never for ten minutes been drama-free. Amanda and Melissa could have had—deserved to have—far better parents. They deserved stability. We didn't have it to give. But we gave them what we had. When we had more, we did not withhold it. When we had less, they were not unscathed. You can't have a father and mother with the kinds of issues Keith and I had and not ride a relentless roller coaster. When we had on seat belts, it was good. It was fun. When we didn't, it was scary. It was sad.

We made some good decisions. We made some god-awful decisions. That we're in one piece, that we're still together, that we love one another beyond the confines of human language is the indelible mark of divine grace. We know it every day of our lives. I have a lot of doubts in this life. Whether or not Jesus tarried with us in our four walls, dispensing mercy like a pharmacist dispenses drugs, is not among them.

We have laughed hard. We have cried hard. We have fought hard.

Some of us have prayed hard. And wondered why on earth everything always had to *be* hard.

Yet there is nothing in the universe I'd trade for having ridden this ride with those two girls.

My daughters. Amanda, Melissa. My sun and my moon. Sunshine, Moonshine.

CHAPTER THIRTEEN

IF IT'S TRUE GOD OFTEN USES THE BODY OF CHRIST—by that I mean a community of fellow believers—to tell us what he wants from us, what he wanted from me in my early twenties was leg warmers. I was a new mom when the aerobics craze took America by sweat and storm. A handful of women at my church decided we needed a class and I was just the person to lead it. *Why,* you ask?

"Didn't you do drill team, Beth?"

"Well, yes, but that's not the same thing as—"

"Fabulous! When's the kickoff?"

In my day, we didn't just *start* things at church. We kicked them off.

"I'm going to have to give this some thought," I explained, "because I promised God that, whatever I did, I'd do as ministry."

Unimpressed, they retorted, "So, do it as ministry."

"How?"

"How are we supposed to know? You figure it out."

I turned the idea over and over in my head, then, when I saw them next, said, "Maybe I could figure a way to use Christian music."

To their credit, they affirmed the idea, though I could plainly see from their expressions that they pictured us stretching in our tights and leotards to "Rock of Ages."

"I need to actually learn how to do aerobics."

Exasperated, they asked, "Well, how long is that gonna take?"

It didn't take long. I enrolled in an aerobics class not far from my home to get the hang of it and, lo and behold, loved it. This was 1980, when Christian contemporary music was just beginning to get airplay on local Christian radio stations. Songs were coming out weekly by artists like Amy Grant, Michael W. Smith, Steven Curtis Chapman, and Leon Patillo, and groups like the Imperials, Petra, Harvest, Farrell and Farrell, and White Heart that were clearly begging for choreography. The music was there if I had enough imagination.

For better and for worse, imagination happens to be one of my strong suits. With a baby on a blanket beside me, kicking her little legs to the beat, I started choreographing aerobic exercises to Christian contemporary music. We announced a kickoff in the church bulletin and on posters in the halls and women's restrooms a month later. The church let us use a small room if we'd remove the chairs ourselves and put them back afterward, and by the first night, we were already short on space.

Eight people was one thing. What's a few lunges between friends? But when the class kept growing, I got antsy. I needed to know what I was doing. I contacted Houston's renowned First

Baptist Church because, according to hearsay, they'd spent a small fortune building, of all scandalous things, what they called a Christian Life Center. It was complete with an indoor track, basketball and racquetball courts, a weight room, a café, a bowling alley, and locker rooms with showers. This was a fancy outfit. A friend of mine had seen the women's locker room with her own eyes and claimed they even furnished handheld hair dryers.

"Wattage?" I asked. This was the true test.

"Twelve hundred."

If any church was going to have personnel who could train me to teach a dance-exercise class as ministry, First Baptist would.

"Now, what is it you're asking again?" The young man on the phone worked the front desk of the CLC, where members could check out a basketball, a pair of bowling shoes, a towel, or the like.

"Could you tell me who is in charge of your women's aerobics program?" My accent was still thick as patty sausage, so I had to repeat the question several times.

"Let me put you through to my boss."

His boss, one of many ministers at FBC, asked me three questions in turn for every one of mine. What kind of class did I teach? How much experience did I have? Had women come back a second and third time? I answered the questions but circled back to my own.

"Sir, what I'm wondering is if you have someone who oversees an aerobics program there?"

"No."

I'd just spent twenty minutes on a phone propped between my ear and my shoulder while I fed the baby a bottle.

"But," he was quick to say, "I'd like to hire one. Would you be interested in applying?"

I'd end up overseeing the program and teaching multiple classes a week—advanced and intermediate—in that "Christian Life Center" for twelve years and cry like there was no tomorrow when the time came to give it up. I've never in my ministry life done anything that was a bigger riot. If pure fun qualified as fruit of the Spirit, we were as Spirit-filled as women in tights get. We laughed and carried on, tripped over our own feet, crunched our stomach muscles, worked our thighs until we felt the burn, danced our hearts out, sang loud to every song, and dripped with enough sweat to swim to the parking lot. Childcare was in a gym, just outside the door in plain sight, where anyone who had kids could drop them off happy as clams. They could run themselves into exhaustion, play games, throw basketballs into miniature hoops and, best of all, learn to roller-skate from Miss Debbie. Those kids became the best roller skaters in the Southern Baptist Convention, bar none. Could Jane Fonda offer that? Could Richard Simmons? Nay, I say.

● ● ●

Ironically, the most important element of my new part-time job was the part I didn't want.

"I'd like you to pray about moving your letter here to First Baptist."

The request came from my new boss moments after he told me I was hired. *Moving your letter* was something Southern Baptists did when we transferred our membership from one church to another. Originally it referred to an actual letter exchanged by the two churches, but over time, the phrase became a bit more figurative. (I ought not have to explain at this point that moving one's letter was activated by walking the aisle at the end of a worship service. After the pastor gave you the right hand of fellowship, you filled out a membership form.)

In our world, it went without saying that moving one's letter was something that occurred laterally between two Southern Baptist churches. If you were moving from a Baptist church to, say, a Methodist church, you were indeed moving somewhere, but it was down. This I write without a whit of meanness. I can't even work up any cynicism. This was our culture, and I was contentedly at home in it. I find comfort in the blessed assurance that other denominations surely had their own forms of exclusivity.

"We prayed about it and feel led to just stay in our neighborhood church," I said to my new boss a week later by phone. I loved our smaller church and had not one inclination to budge, hair dryers or no hair dryers. The other line went silent for about fifteen seconds, then he said, "Well, then, I may not have made the offer as clear as I should have. I apologize for that. It's part of the offer. I hope that's not too inconvenient."

I was aghast and went to Keith immediately and intoned to him the audacity.

"Fine with me," he said, shrugging his shoulders. "I'd ten times rather be somewhere we can get lost in the crowd."

That I can't recall the speech I gave Keith in response is a shame. No way it didn't include a fusion of biblical threats like "Well, if you want to hide your light under a bushel and forfeit your salt, then stand before the judgment seat, go right ahead."

I took this crisis with great haste to the Lord in prayer, to which the Lord responded with equal haste by moving our letter to First Baptist Church. I've found that walking by faith is 50 percent hanging in there until you're far enough down the road to develop hindsight. I cannot think of one thing God appears to have done more strategically than move Keith and me to First Baptist. The opportunities that would start coming my way as a result were by no means based on my credibility. I hadn't had time to build any.

I also wasn't unique in any way nor, that I could tell, particularly talented. The opportunities came to me based on the credibility of my church and its pastor, John Bisagno.

If there is any such thing as a life-pastor—one you'd say marked your life the longest and deepest and for good, mind you, and not for evil—unquestionably, John Bisagno would be mine. I'd remain under his leadership until he retired just short of twenty years later. He was a concoction of strengths and weaknesses just like the rest of us, but I've never met anyone who found more unquenchable joy in helping men *and women* do what God had called them to do. Brother John's ego bowed low to his eagerness to see people thrive in Jesus. He sought out the most gifted young preachers on the landscape to speak from his pulpit, knowing good and well he'd be compared to them. Didn't care. If he had to divest himself of power in order to invest in the next generation, fine with him.

My first official opportunity to stand in front of a group and speak occurred at First Baptist's annual women's retreat when I was still in my early twenties. I'd been asked to do a breakout session on, you guessed it, aerobics. All my earliest speaking invitations were tied to this topic. I entitled the fifty-minute message "Making Fitness Count for Christ." I spoke for the first thirty, then slapped a cassette tape in my boom box and got them on their feet the last twenty. Granted, the choreography had to be carefully crafted to accommodate attire since, in those days, most women came to church retreats at fancy hotels in dresses and navy-blue hosiery.

I'd like to interject at this moment that writing this memoir has been, at certain points, like being skinned alive by vile demons with a potato peeler. I've endured for moments like this one. The gift our young selves give to our old selves, if we're lucky, is pure absurdity. I have hated the young woman I used to be many times for many reasons, but I can only love a woman who takes herself seriously reading from a Bible while wearing a sweatband. Give me this.

At the end of the first of a jillion breakout sessions I'd do in my young speaking life, a woman named Marge Caldwell approached me. I knew who she was. Everybody at the women's retreat knew who she was. Among the sages of Houston's First Baptist Church, warm and charming and funny, she was probably the most popular Christian motivational speaker in our denomination even at almost seventy. Women speakers in the conservative church world were only slightly scarcer than unicorns. Marge had served all over the United States and in multiple foreign countries. She was the keynote speaker at the retreat.

The embodiment of grace and poise, Marge reached out her hand and introduced herself to me.

"Yes, yes, ma'am, I know who you are, Mrs. Caldwell."

"Call me Marge," she said. I nodded but didn't. We'd soon become as thick as blood and still I'd struggle to call her by her first name.

"Beth," she said, her blue eyes narrowing, "I think you're called to do this."

I assumed she meant teaching aerobics. I felt a bead of sweat run from under my thick hair down my spine.

"No, no, I don't mean *this* so much," she quickly followed up, shooting a glance toward my three-pound hand weights. "I mean, I think you're called to speak."

• • •

Every now and then God sends a prophetic word to one servant through another that has no immediate effect or manifestation.

It's meant to be pondered humbly, not broadcasted publicly. It's intended to be planted like seed in the fertile soil of the heart, deeply enough where the birds of prey can't peck it away. Those words can't be forced to fruition, though we will inevitably try, even when we're warned of the futility. I gave the Lord a little time then decided he must be waiting for me to take initiative. I talked Keith into springing the money for printing a tricolor flyer with my picture on it. The blurb below it read, "Elizabeth Moore, professional Christian Speaker and Teacher, is a welcomed addition to the world of Christian motivators and communicators."

I wrote the blurb. Indeed, I welcomed myself. I sent them to every church I could find in the yellow pages within a ten-mile radius, and for the life of me, I cannot recall a solitary result. It is possible the Lord hid them. A stack of expensive tricolor flyers is in a box somewhere in my attic, the supply having severely exceeded the demand. That I'd capitalized *Speaker* and *Teacher* might have some bearing on the humbling that would come in my thirties.

A seed needs planting in order to grow. It needs patience. If the seed was cast from the hand of God, he will surely sprout it, in his time, in his way. If it came from good human intentions, consider it no waste. It was a mortal's vocalized belief that you have something to offer, and while that person may prove mistaken about the precise form, that faith can act as fertilizer to the soil.

Marge Caldwell had her own journey in a world of podiums, in a day when our honorarium might amount to a corsage we wore while speaking, wondering if the pin was going to pop a breast like a balloon. Men don't have to worry about these things. Fitness wasn't the gateway topic that first brought Marge to a podium. Her intro was poise and manners, the former of which entailed how to stand and sit properly and how to find the right dress style for your God-given shape. She somehow managed to do this without a whiff of body shaming. Her manners classes, on the other hand, ranged all the way from making proper introductions when hosting a dinner party to knowing a salad fork from a dessert fork. You weren't well acquainted with Marge Caldwell if you didn't know which plate to put your dinner roll on. Let the bread basket pass you by.

In those days and in that world, invitations to speak only about Jesus were rare. Think of it this way. Most of what we did was speak at teas. You couldn't speak at a tea and serve it up straight. The first cups had to be mostly milk and sugar, and you'd better serve good cookies.

Several years after my introduction to Marge, I seized the first opportunity to serve my tea straight. I was still teaching aerobics and would continue to for seven more years. Don't imagine I'd spoken for the last time on "Making Fitness Count for Christ." Christian women were heavily invested in leotards by this time. The taste of Jesus was on my tongue now, however, and there would be no washing it down.

I was twenty-seven years old, Amanda and Melissa five and two, when the phone rang, and Marge's voice sounded on the other end. Her voice had become as familiar to me by now as honey and butter on a warm biscuit.

"First Baptist needs a substitute Sunday school teacher for married women in the young adult department. It would just be for a year while the regular teacher takes a maternity break. I told them I thought I knew exactly who should do it."

The thing about active mentors who have poured untold energy into you is how famously difficult it is to say no to them. I stammered around. I was no stranger to teaching Sunday school, but only to children. I was speaking by now at women's events on a fairly frequent basis, and with five messages in my repertoire, I could recycle indefinitely and save myself hours of preparation time. Why would I also want to teach Sunday school?

In my most deferential voice, I responded, "Well, you know, with the speaking and all, I'm not sure how it would work."

"Now, you may speak more than I do, Beth," she said as sweet as molasses, both of us knowing full well I didn't speak a tenth as often as she did, "but doing them both has worked for me for twenty years. In fact, they work well together."

I needn't waste ink expounding on how few days passed before I was teaching Sunday school to a group of married women twenty-eight to thirty-one years of age. I was the youngest person in the class. I dreaded every Sunday like a tooth extraction. I'd have been better off reading aloud the Sunday school quarterly which, at that time, held all the excitement of an obituary. Instead, I had the bright idea to freestyle and think up what I wanted to talk about and, come Saturday, have a near panic attack scrambling to find a Bible verse to go with it. I was terrible. That's not to say I wasn't fun. We had fun all right. We just didn't learn anything about the Bible. You can't deliver Sunday school lessons as motivational speeches and manage to disciple people.

The end of the year couldn't come quickly enough. I resolved never to darken the door of another Sunday school class in a teaching capacity.

•   •   •

One Sunday morning about ten miserable months into my teaching commitment, I was sitting in the worship center beside Keith, waiting for the service to begin and miserable yet again over the inspirational talk I'd just substituted for a Bible lesson. As the organist played and our spectacular two-hundred-voice choir filed into the loft, I sighed with self-contempt and distracted myself with the bulletin. Announcements of upcoming events were on the back.

A new class on Bible doctrine begins in two weeks during the Training Union hour in room 235, taught by Buddy Walters.

The Lord bid me *GO. For the love of all things holy, go.*

I didn't know the teacher from Adam. What I knew was that I'd be bored to tears, but at least I'd learn something. I prepared for the sacrifice by motivating myself with a clean new spiral notebook—college ruled—and a package of colored pens and the obligatory yellow highlighter. Around fifteen of us showed up, and as well as I'm able to recall, the class didn't grow significantly larger. Training Union, after all, was on Sunday evenings for an hour before another church service. This was discipleship for diehards.

Buddy Walters had a quiet presence. A former college-football player, he was as thick as he was wide—one contiguous muscle—but surprisingly unassuming, like he had no idea what a presence he was. There was no fanfare in his class, not even for the kickoff. No *let's go around the room and introduce ourselves.* When the clock struck 6:00 p.m., he plainly walked to the podium in the small Sunday school room, flopped open a king-size KJV and told us to turn to Genesis. I'd never seen a Bible in worse condition.

The man bowed his head and asked the Lord to use him, then launched into a lesson without bell or whistle. He didn't have a booming voice. He didn't even use a lot of inflection. His deep voice and long drawl stayed steady and authoritative even at times when tears mystifyingly pooled in his eyes. He'd not told a sad story or anything. He just taught, shifting back and forth between the podium and the chalkboard. Each time he added an item to the Bible chart he'd drawn, he clapped a plume of chalk dust off his hands and flipped another page of his Bible. I don't recall turning pages that first night or taking down notes. All I remember is sitting, mesmerized.

I'd never seen a person like Buddy. I'd never met anyone who seemed to study the Bible for the sheer delight of it and not simply the discipline. I appreciated the Bible. Respected it. Embraced a way of living and talking that developed from it. But I didn't *love* it. Not like that guy loved it.

The second he closed in prayer, I stood up from my chair, grabbed my purse, and walked straight out the door without a word. Instead of staying for the service, I walked quickly down the stairs and through the hall and out the door to the massive parking lot as fast as I could. I ran to my car, threw my purse in the passenger seat, got in, shut the door, and burst into tears. "I don't know what that was," I cried to God, leaning forward toward the windshield in case he couldn't see me through the roof, "but I want it."

There are not many parts of my life story that make me cry nearly every time I tell them, but this one does. We can't always define what we yearn for in Christ. We don't even know such sacred affections are possible for regular run-of-the-mill humans like us until we see it in someone else.

That night in the car, I suppose before I even turned the ignition, God, in effect, struck a match against a stone and lit a torch in my heart for the Scriptures that has never been quenched. The intensity of the flames rises and recedes from day to day, but in thirty-five years, the fire God set within me that evening has never gone out. I didn't deserve it or earn it. I don't really even understand it, but I've yet to get my fill of Bible study. I'll come to a sudden realization how two scenes in Scripture connect and still slap my desk over it.

I'd spend several years under Buddy's teaching. I was ravenous. I became such a pest, interrupting class with questions, that he began assigning me homework.

"You can't already be finished with that," he'd say.

"Yes, I am! See?" and I'd show him the completed assignments.

He made appointments to come to our house to teach me how to use Bible commentaries and dictionaries. A stickler for propriety, Buddy made my husband sit at the table with us. Keith would flip through *Field and Stream* while Buddy and I flipped through Bible resources, and the more Keith learned about fishing, the more I learned about teaching. I'd teach Sunday school nonstop for the next twenty-three years, and Marge would be proven right, of course. Studying for roughly forty-five to fifty Sunday school lessons a year for adults, one book of the Bible after another, would break the Bible wide open into endless topics, themes, and messages that would feed decades of events on the road.

Other mentors would come into my life for a season or a particular purpose, but these three—Brother John, Marge, and Buddy—remain unrivaled in influence. Each made a deep indentation, a bold point with a permanent marker. Draw lines connecting them, and they form a triangle that shaped my entire ministry life. Brother John's insatiable desire to see individuals come to Jesus and discover what he'd called them to do was infectious. Marge's love for being a woman and for serving and defending women multiplies like blood cells in my bone marrow. Buddy's passion for the Scriptures ruined me for anything but a life of study.

Within the sturdy triangle they built around me, I would slowly find my own way of being and walking and living and talking with Jesus. I'd find my own way of teaching. As God would often have it, I believe, the thumbprints of multiple mentors pressed into the clay of a life shapes a certain distinctiveness. You're too much a mix of all of them to turn out just like any one of them. To these three, all of whom now stand in God's presence, I owe a debt impossible to repay.

CHAPTER FOURTEEN

THE TEACHING MINISTRY to which I'd give the name Living Proof grew up with my daughters, not only in time but in form, with all the tumbles and falls that go with toddlerhood and the scrapes, near misses, speeding tickets, fender benders, and driving through stop signs accompanying life on wheels. I can't say the ministry has grown up nearly as well as Amanda and Melissa have, nor that its growing was always *up*, but similarities abound.

By the time my girls were climbing aboard Big Wheels, I was climbing aboard airplanes, adapting to a world of seat belts, tray tables, and overhead compartments. Keith and I figured out a travel schedule we could manage without pulling one another's hair out, and I started traveling two Friday nights a month, rarely back-to-back, while Keith held down the fort.

No two parents parent identically. Keith's way of holding down the fort was not my way since I was substantially more weak-kneed to the girls' whims. They could talk me into just about anything. Keith, on the other hand, was bound and determined not to be a pushover. Though he is one of the most generous individuals I've ever known, Keith is infamous in our family for choosing unique places to draw the line. I'd call home to see how things were going.

"Mom, come home! Dad won't even let us get cheese on a hamburger at the drive-through when you are out of town!"

"Put your father on the phone." I'd hear grumbling and grousing.

"Hello?" Keith would say in his John Moore Plumbing Company voice, like I was a customer with a clogged toilet.

"Babe, for crying out loud, why won't you let the girls get cheese on their hamburgers?"

"Because it's ten cents extra, and they can slap a slice of American cheese on it when we get home."

We never could sort out this conflict. "It's a matter of principle," he'd say.

"What principle?" I'd say.

"You can't just give them everything they want! That's not how life is!"

"Keith, it's *cheese*."

And it was. But it also wasn't. He was right about me. I did want them to have most everything they wanted, and my idea of him holding down the fort was doing whatever they asked. Mind you, Keith could be great fun, but when I was out of town, the good times were going to roll down his lane. He'd often treat them to a movie or laze around with them all Saturday morning in front of cartoons. But sometimes he felt the best way he and the girls could bond on a Saturday with Mom away was by cleaning out the garage he'd been needing to cull for eighteen months, and boy, was I going to hear about it.

We four made it work, not perfectly by any stretch of the imagination, but well enough to stay in one piece, and we kept that same schedule for years. I wanted to work. Keith wanted me to work. We needed the money, and by now, I was beginning to get honorariums for women's retreats that exceeded the cost of a tank of gas.

There's no having it all. That's an undeniable fact. But I wanted two things desperately. I wanted my family, and I wanted ministry. I wanted to raise my own children. I also wanted women to catch a fever for the Scriptures. I loved being home, and I loved being on the road. I adored my two little girls, and I also adored cracking open a Bible with a room full of females. To their credit—Keith, Amanda, and Melissa's—alongside ocean tides of grace, I've had those two things. How well they balanced from day to day was up for grabs, but both were constants.

What fell entirely through the cracks was my social life. Friendships that weren't built into the family construct through church, neighborhood, or the kids' schools or sports circled the drain. They were not small losses but necessary. Something had to go. Nothing about balancing family and ministry worked perfectly. I can't even say it consistently worked smoothly, but it worked well enough for us to make it.

Ministry is tough on a family. Imagine feeling like you're competing with God for your primary person's affections. The opportunity for people in vocational ministry to spiritually manipulate those around them is lake-wide. Slender is the bridge above it. I attempted to keep my feet affixed, but the path could get slippery, and goodness knows no deception is slyer than self-deception. To whatever degree I didn't use God against my family, Keith deserves substantial credit, cheese or no cheese. A plumber by trade, his nose for sniffing out manure and his mouth for calling it were effective deterrents. Who knows how much difficulty ministry added to the family mix? It's all we ever knew.

Notoriety is a different matter. We four know precisely how much stress that added to the mix, but I'll get to that later.

• • •

Our family dynamics extended beyond the four humans under our roof. Our lives were tightly braided pigtails with each set of our children's grandparents. Except for the earliest years of our marriage, Keith worked with his dad at the plumbing company. We were in and out of his parents' home continually and met them at restaurants every chance we got. Keith's dad was no fool. He knew the best way to maintain a close relationship with his married children was to offer a meal out and foot the bill. We and Keith's siblings and their young families would show up at the drop of a hat.

As for the Green side of our family, no amount of difficulty or distraction could pry my siblings or me from my mom. Gay and I always lived within short driving distance of our parents, but even our other siblings who moved away never stayed away long. None of us were ever out of touch with her, or for that matter, with Dad, since they were a package deal. These were not uncomplicated dynamics for some of us, but a family can go a long way on denial. The maddening complexity is, denial could, on occasion, offer a little relief. It makes for a poor lifestyle but a pleasant lunch.

By this time, another grenade, bigger than ever, had dropped in our family over my father's past transgressions, so the joys my parents found during my college years had been cut short. They would never recover from this one, though they'd stay married and in church and make all the obligatory appearances, and each stayed present in our family. The ice thawed somewhat through the years, but the sun never really came out between them again. Their domains were separate enough anyway. Dad still worked movie theater hours and, even when he was around, tended to live in a bit of a bubble. Mom had the run of the house and the television. She had her soap operas, her flower beds, her letter-writing, her afternoon naps, and, most precious to her of all, a revolving door for her children and grandchildren.

When I think back, I marvel at how much life took place under those overcast skies at my parents' house. Some of my favorite memories of Mom are woven into the years my girls were young. Aletha hit and missed a bit as a mother. Hit, I want to say, more than missed. But she was the finest grandmother I ever knew. My mother was at her best in the company of her grandchildren. This was true from the firstborn among them to the last. She was a Rountree, after all, drunk on babies. She played with them on the floor even when she got so frail, we'd have to help her up. She rocked them a thousand miles. Gay and I had young families at the same time, and our idea of bliss was being together with Mom. She read to our children, talked incessantly to them, and drew vocabulary out of them that constantly entertained us. She wooed them into a world of stories and scenes, of dress-ups, masquerades, and families made of clay.

The movie E.T.: The Extra-Terrestrial was booming at the box office when Amanda was three and four years old, and she became obsessed with the hairless, bug-eyed fictional creature at its center. We were at Mom's one day when I came in from the backyard and couldn't find either one of them. After calling for them multiple times, I heard a familiar little girl's giggle coming from inside the hall closet. I opened the door to find Mom's and Amanda's faces surrounded by stuffed animals like a scene from the movie. This was my mom. She made every ordinary thing magic to my children. She bought them frocks from Kmart that, to them, may as well have come from Neiman Marcus. She created a space on a low budget where a Salisbury-steak frozen dinner was eating high on the hog. She sang more in hoarse chords than melodies on account of all the Marlboros, but the definition of glee to Amanda and Melissa was singing songs with their nanny. That's what they called her.

Nanny.

"I love you, Nanny!" Arms so tight around her neck, the vein on her forehead bulged.

She'd smooch them big on the cheek with every bit of lip she could roll out and say effortlessly to them what she felt with all her heart but struggled to articulate to my siblings and me. "I love you, too." Just like that. Just like it was how we all talked in our family.

I love you, a bushel and a peck
A bushel and a peck and a hug around the neck

I never resented how her grandparenting exceeded her parenting. I beamed, feeling like most mothers do. You want to know how to love me? Love my children. You want to be good to me? Be good to my children.

She was their best friend. Any of my siblings who lived close enough for her to be continually involved in their children's lives would say the same. We would also say she was ours. I can't think of a single slice of our existence characterized by ease, but many of these days were especially good days.

● ● ●

Our four-Moore, four-pet, tight-budget family was making it somewhat stably amid our steady stream of conflicts and challenges when, soon after I turned thirty, we made one of the most monumental decisions of our lives. Keith's younger cousin had a four-year-old son she was unable to parent due to the relentless battering of a drug addiction. Her dad, Keith's paternal uncle, and his new wife had taken the child in and done the best they could, but the situation was unsustainable. The genetics on Keith's side of the family are bold and unapologetic, especially among the males. This little guy, who I'd never seen, was rumored to be my husband's spitting image. To Keith, seeing the boy was like seeing himself at four years old. And seeing himself at four years old, the embers of the house fire still burning and skin still blistering, was nearly unbearable.

"We could take him in," he said. "What's one more?"

The thing was, our youngest had just found her feet in elementary school. I loved my girls' infancies, toddlerhoods, and preschool years, and I cried like a baby their first days of kindergarten, but having given those years my all and from the get-go of marriage, school-bus yellow had become my new favorite color. I was wet-faced with a sudsy, fresh wave of freedom. I could accomplish all kinds of work during school hours and still be standing on the front lawn, smiling ear to ear, when the bus driver ground the brakes at my curb every weekday afternoon.

"I just don't know, honey. That's a lot. Three children are substantially more than two."

My mom had always claimed it was so. She said she never regretted having five, but that a parent was outnumbered the moment she had more children than hands.

Keith kept bringing him up. I kept needing more time to think.

A few months later, we spent all day Saturday at an extended Moore family picnic at a park in Houston, and my gaze fell on the loveliest little boy. Dark hair, big brown eyes.

"Whose child is that?" I whispered in Keith's ear while he gnawed a pork rib clean. He dropped it on his paper plate, cleared the baked beans from his throat, and said his cousin's name, motioning toward his uncle trailing a dozen or so feet behind the boy.

"That's *him*?"

"Yep," Keith replied.

"That's the little boy you've been talking about?"

"Yep."

"Can't be. That child couldn't possibly be four years old."

"Yeah, he is. He's just small. He needs a lot."

That beautiful little boy would move into our home shortly after. All four of us had stars in our eyes. A little brother sounded marvelous to Amanda and Melissa. A son sounded marvelous to Keith, especially one who favored him so. And then there was me with the loftiest thoughts of all. I recall saying the words out loud, "Let's love him to wholeness."

It's hard to love someone to a place you've never been.

We nicknamed him Spud. Thinking he was ours forever, we tried right away to adopt him, but his mom's whereabouts remained unknown and his father wouldn't sign the papers. He sought no role in the boy's life, but he seemed strangely empowered by controlling the legalities. It wasn't a grudge against us. We'd never met. Perhaps it was just a grudge against life in general.

Legal guardianship transferred from Spud's grandparents to us, and we embraced him as our own. I've given this a torturous amount of thought in hindsight. Should we have ever taken on the

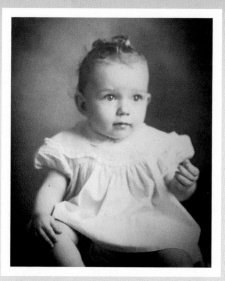

Me at 9 months old

My darling mom (center) in 1960

My dad and me

Nanny, Mom, my siblings, and me

The five of us (from left): me, Gay, Wayne, Tony, and Sandra

The three little ones: Gay, Tony, and me

Christmas 1961

Senior Prom. My mom made my
dress and I loved it!

Practicing piano with the maestro (Wayne)
over my head in 1962

Keith duck hunting, 1980

Our honeymoon, 1978

The five of us on Easter 1987: Keith,
Amanda, Melissa, me and my hair

My baby girls: Sunshine (right) and Moonshine (left)

Amanda's wedding

Melissa and me, May 2019

Living Proof
Live (above
and right)

Receiving an honorary doctorate from Gordon College in 2019

An impromptu Q&A with Keith at a Living Proof Live event in 2006

Our home in the woods

Keith, our bird dog Creek, and me, 2021

names Mom and Dad and called the girls his sisters, or should we have insisted on Uncle Keith, Aunt Beth, and cousins Amanda and Melissa? There never seems to be a crystal ball when you need one. Spud wanted a family. He didn't want cousins. He asked within a week of being in our home if he could call me Mom. I stuttered around, trying to think of the right answer and ultimately didn't have the heart to say no. The way I saw it, plenty of stepmothers, mothers-in-law, and mother figures went by *Mom*. And I was willing. I was more than willing. I was *determined*. As determined as I have ever been about anything in my life.

Spud's needs differed greatly from our girls'. They were doing fine in public school. We knew early on he'd require private education. We knew he needed medical help and sought it. We knew his heart was fractured, and we set out to be used by God to mend it. Through no fault of his, we would ultimately prove unable to do so. He was worth much more than we had to offer.

Created in the image of God, we humans, by and large, have an inherent desire to save. We want so badly to rescue. Understandably, our little guy's needs were great. By sheer necessity, the girls had to take a back seat to our new family member. They still loved him. We all did. We desperately wanted ours to be the perfect home for him. He had been through so much in his short life. Abandonment by both parents is a heck of a thing. The child's ability to attach can be woefully compromised. The bonding Keith pictured would not materialize as he hoped, a reality he'd find devastating.

Despite the challenges, we bought in, withholding nothing we had to give. We did all the regular things with our fifth family member that we'd done with four—school, sports, church, grandparents, aunts, uncles, cousins, trips, summers at the neighborhood pool, bikes, vacations, Moore and Green Christmases and holidays. Like hosts of other families, whatever successes we enjoyed were three steps forward and two steps back. I'm no math wizard, but as far as I could count, one step was still forward. I'd joke that I was a mom of six: Amanda was the equivalent of one child, Melissa, two, and Spud, at the very least, three.

Spud and I spent weekdays together, just the two of us, while his sisters were in school and Keith was at work. He went with me to the Christian Life Center three times a week, where I taught aerobics and he learned to roller-skate just like the girls had. Eighteen months later, my brown-eyed potato went to a carefully selected private kindergarten thirty minutes from our home.

He was a challenge to his teachers from the start, so I did what I had to do. I set out to make sure he was the cutest one in his class. I'd like to go on record saying that, having failed at a thousand other things, I am confident of having succeeded in this. The boy never went to school a single day under my care without hair product. He was adorable—and don't tell me adorable doesn't matter when it comes to a difficult child. The principal, a capable and godly woman if I'd ever met one, called me nearly every week. The range of Spud's misdeeds widely varied. Some of them were serious and mystifying. We were doing everything we knew to do, seeking multiple avenues of professional help, while also trying to parent two other children. The tears and frustrations were innumerable. Baffled, I'd sometimes say to him, "Son, why on earth did you do that?"

He didn't know. He really didn't.

When he was in the second grade, I was asked to come early for afternoon car pool because the principal needed a few minutes. My heart sank. I knew this drill. I also knew how hard the school was trying. From start to finish, they were never anything but fair with us. This time Spud had needed to go to the bathroom